WALES
CASTLES
& HISTORIC PLACES

Llanthony Priory by J.M.W. Turner, 1775–1851 (By courtesy of the Trustees of the British Museum).

WALES
CASTLES
& HISTORIC PLACES

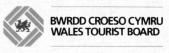

BWRDD CROESO CYMRU
WALES TOURIST BOARD

Cadw
WELSH
HISTORIC
MONUMENTS

Published by Wales Tourist Board and Cadw: Welsh Historic Monuments, Brunel House, 2 Fitzalan Road, CARDIFF CF2 1UY.
© Wales Tourist Board — Cadw: Welsh Historic Monuments

First Published in 1990

Written and edited by David M. Robinson and Roger S. Thomas

Designed by Rhian Davies and Judith Armstrong

Typeset by Afal Typesetting

Colour Processing by Severn Studios

Printed in Great Britain by Artisan Press

ISBN 1 85013 030 2

WALES
CASTLES
& HISTORIC PLACES

CONTENTS

Dolbadarn Castle by J.M.W. Turner, 1775-1851 (By courtesy of the Royal Academy of Arts).

WALES
THROUGH THE AGES

INTRODUCTION

W ales, we are so often told, is a land of castles. Even to the newcomer, it is not difficult to see why. From the lush valleys of the eastern and southern borderlands — the March — to the rugged heart of the mountainous north and west, picturesque silhouettes of castles enhance an already engaging landscape. With names as famous as Caernarfon and Harlech, Kidwelly and Pembroke, or Chepstow and Raglan, these treasured remnants of the Middle Ages are familiar to both residents and visitors alike.

If we pause for a moment though, and look a little more deeply into the Welsh countryside, it soon becomes clear that castles are just one part of a rich inheritance of ancient and historic sites — a legacy as rich and varied as that of any part of the British Isles. Indeed, in a region where nature's stage — the physical landscape — offers such attractive and widely contrasting possibilities, it comes as no surprise to learn that Wales has witnessed an unbroken chain of settlement from the dawn of history beyond. Throughout the Principality, man has left tell-tale signs, in the form of numerous monuments, of all ages. They bear testimony to aspects of daily life such as custom, ritual and burial, to phases of ruthless military conquest and peaceful occupation, and even to dramatically changing cultures and physical conditions.

This little book is a guide to some of the more readily accessible examples of these monuments and historic sites, principally those in the care of Cadw: Welsh Historic Monuments, the National Trust, and other bodies concerned with the heritage of Wales. As might be expected, it concentrates on the great castles of the Middle Ages, but also provides insights into a much older past. Moreover, moving forward from the age of castles, Wales has many fine examples of fortified mansions and later country houses — these, too, are covered in the extensive gazetteer.

The brief survey of Wales through the ages which follows is offered by way of introduction. It is not intended as an overall historical survey, since the range of themes and span are far too extensive to cover in so short a space. Rather, it explores the essential characteristics of the monuments themselves. As such, it should help visitors using the gazetteer to place any particular site in a much broader chronological and geographical framework.

A handaxe from Rhossili, on the Gower Peninsula. This is one of the oldest stone tools found in Wales, lost or left by its owner about 125,000 years ago (By permission of the National Museum of Wales).

Flint tools from Paviland Cave on the Gower Peninsula (By permission of the National Museum of Wales).

WALES BC

A reconstruction drawing of the burial of the 'Red Lady' of Paviland. The bones were in fact those of a young man, stained red or orange by the ochre deposited with the body (By permission of the National Museum of Wales).

A reconstruction drawing of how people may have lived about 9,000 years ago during the Middle Stone Age. Small groups would have survived by moving from camp to camp, hunting game, gathering plants and fishing (By permission of the National Museum of Wales).

The story of man in Wales can now be traced back as far as 250,000 BC, to a cave site at Pontnewydd in Clwyd. As well as simple stone 'tools', this important site has yielded fragments of human bone, believed to belong to 'Neanderthal Man' — one of our primitive ancestors — and hailed in this instance as 'the first Welshman'!

It is not until almost the closing stages of the 'Ice Age' that we begin to discern growing numbers of sites occupied by man. One of the most famous and intriguing later Old Stone Age locations is Paviland Cave on the Gower peninsula. Bones found there in the 19th century and thought to be those of the celebrated 'Red Lady', were in fact those of a young man. One theory holds that he was buried some 30,000 years ago, just before the last major advance of the ice sheets; but 'radio-carbon' dating suggests that he may have been one of a hunting party on the fringes of the glaciers, about 16,500 BC.

Around 8,000-7,000 BC, as the ice cap gradually retreated northwards for the last time, bands of hunters and fishermen settled around the shores of the rising post-glacial sea. Burry Holms on Gower and Nab Head in Dyfed are sites where stone tools and weapons of these so-called Mesolithic (Middle Stone Age) communities have been found.

The prehistory of Wales assumes increasing clarity from Neolithic (New Stone Age) times, about 4,000-2,000 BC, certainly in terms of monuments which survive in significant numbers in the landscape. It was during this period that the 'first farmers' made their appearance. These early agricultural groups initiated fundamental changes in man's relationship with his surroundings by cultivating crops and taming livestock thus tying people to more specific areas of land, so promoting a more settled way of life. Curiously, however, the actual settlements of these communities are very difficult to identify, and the monuments which we can see today — 'cromlechs' — were connected primarily with burial and religious ceremonies. These megalithic tombs were often constructed of large boulders set on end, and covered with massive capstones. Although their details vary, examples of them are scattered across Wales, from Tinkinswood in the south-east or Pentre Ifan in the west, to the notable and wide-ranging group on the Isle of Anglesey.

Towards the end of the Neolithic, many of these chambered tombs passed out of use. Gradually, changes in society led to the introduction of new forms of monument, possibly reflecting increased ceremonial activity. The structures we now call 'henges' made their first appearance at this time. Characterized by their construction in the shape of a roughly circular bank and internal ditch, they probably served as ritual enclosures. The earliest examples, including that identified at Bryn Celli Ddu on Anglesey, were simple, bearing little of the eventual elaboration seen, for instance, at Stonehenge in Wiltshire. This period also saw the emergence of 'passage graves' in north-west Wales. A superb example can be seen at Barclodiad y Gawres on the west coast of Anglesey, and another which superseded the henge at Bryn Celli Ddu.

The Neolithic tradition of large communal tombs seems to have declined by about 2,000 BC, with widespread change to individual burial. This coincides with the introduction of new and distinct forms of pottery, known as 'beakers'. The idea of an invasion of 'Beaker Folk', is no longer accepted, and instead it is suggested that beakers formed part of a 'cult package' in which ideas and objects linked to central beliefs (originating somewhere on the Continent) spread relatively rapidly, but without major movements of people. Nor can we be sure that the introduction of metal objects was associated with the beaker phenomenon. Nevertheless, the gradual occurrence of metalware — copper at first, but later bronze — heralds the period still called for convenience the Bronze Age.

Beakers are still seen as prestige vessels, and their presence in individual graves seems to indicate a growing trend towards an acknowledgement of individual power. This willingness to place precious objects of stone, pottery and even gold in graves presumably reflects the wealth and status of the dead. Indeed, it would be difficult to parallel the conspicuous splendour seen in the cape of beaten gold found at Mold in Clwyd.

By 1,500 BC the range of burial sites and ritual practices in Wales, as elsewhere in Britain, was immense, and presents us with a bewildering array of customs and traditions which are difficult to interpret. Although not particularly prominent individually, earthen barrows and stone cairns exist in most areas. Those which have been excavated reveal that cremation was virtually universal in burials at this time. In some cases, mounds were raised over single burials, in others they covered multiple interments. Moreover, not all cairns had a primary burial function, and we should be aware of a broader spectrum of interrelated ritual and belief. Ceremonial monuments, too, continued to feature in the landscape, though their character had changed. Stone rings and standing stones reveal an emphasis upon the forces of life and nature, rather than the concern for death and ancestors seen in the Neolithic.

Unfortunately, it is difficult to trace developments in the later Bronze Age in terms of monuments, and most of the

A reconstruction drawing of a Neolithic ritual burial in the chambered tomb at Tinkinswood, South Glamorgan (Illustration by Alan Sorrell, by permission of the National Museum of Wales).

One of the elaborately carved stones from the 'passage grave' at Barclodiad y Gawres, Anglesey.

The central chamber inside the reconstructed 'passage grave' at Barclodiad y Gawres. The cremated remains of only two people were found inside the tomb, perhaps reflecting the changing emphasis from communal to individual burial.

A Beaker pot from Llanharry, Glamorgan. This carefully decorated pot accompanied the crouched skeleton of a man buried beneath an earthen round barrow (By permission of the National Museum of Wales).

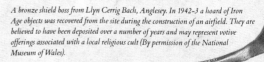

A bronze shield boss from Llyn Cerrig Bach, Anglesey. In 1942-3 a hoard of Iron Age objects was recovered from the site during the construction of an airfield. They are believed to have been deposited over a number of years and may represent votive offerings associated with a local religious cult (By permission of the National Museum of Wales).

Parc le Breos chambered tomb on the Gower Peninsula. The remains of up to 40 people were recovered from this Neolithic mass burial site.

An aerial view of the Iron Age hillfort of Caerau, near Llantrisant. Settlement evidence increases dramatically in the Iron Age with the development of defended hilltop enclosures. Smaller sites like Caerau may indicate the emergence of a local constructional tradition (By courtesy of the Glamorgan-Gwent Archaeological Trust).

A bronze plaque from Llyn Cerrig Bach, (By permission of the National Museum of Wales).

evidence in Wales comes from finds of metalwork. The size of the bronze industry had grown considerably, and by about 1,000 BC the preponderance of weapons among this metalwork reveals a distinct warrior element in society. Growing friction, probably stemming from competition for land resources, partly explains this increase in weaponry, and stress is further emphasized by the appearance of defended hilltop enclosures. It is now clear that hillforts — thought to originate in the Iron Age — were known in the later Bronze Age, though their existence was probably short-lived at this stage.

A renewed phase of hillfort building, together with a steady increase in finds of early ironwork, marks the advent of the Iron Age itself, around 600 BC. In contrast to the burial sites of the Neolithic and Bronze Age, hillforts in particular now become the chief indicators of human settlement. There is, however, considerable variety in the form and construction of these walled or embanked enclosures, which may reflect significant regional differences in society. In the Marches and along the northern seaboard, there are numerous large and strongly defended sites. Dinas Brân near Llangollen, Ffridd Faldwyn near Montgomery, Tre'r Ceiri on the Lleyn peninsula, or even Caer y Twr on Holyhead mountain, impress by their sheer might. The forts in the south and south-west are generally much smaller. Moreover, although some are strongly fortified, others can hardly have been sited with military considerations chiefly in mind.

Archaeologists have so far failed to agree on the extent to which an influx of new peoples influenced developments in Iron Age Britain. As some point out, Celtic was established as a new language during the period, and this may have been linked to immigrations by small numbers of people possessing military power and a strong centralized organization. It may well be these people who were responsible for the distinct hillfort architecture in north-east Wales. Others, however, prefer to see the roots of Iron Age regionalism in the later Bronze Age and talk of a 'cumulative Celticity', a gradual build up of a Celtic culture over a very long period.

Whatever the case, there must have been an interchange between the various cultures in the last 400-500 years before the arrival of the Roman legions, leading, for example to the range of hillfort types in south-east Wales, some of which reveal more than one phase of building over several centuries.

By the eve of the Roman conquest, regional differences in Iron Age Wales had become consolidated in the form of tribal areas. The north-east was occupied by the *Cornovii* and *Deceangli*, with the *Ordovices* in the north-west. The *Demetae* were located in the south-west, and finally the south-east was controlled by the *Silures*.

THE INFLUENCE OF ROME

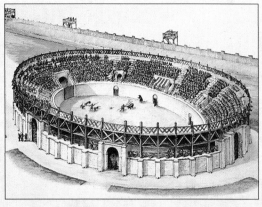

The peaceful remains of the first century Roman amphitheatre at Caerleon belie the bustle of activity that would have echoed from the packed stadium as shown in the imaginary reconstruction drawing. The arena would have been the scene of military training and ruthless sports including the notorious gladitorial combat.

*B*ritish prehistory was effectively brought to an end by the conquests of the Roman legions in the years following AD 43. However, despite a rapid advance across southern England, it took them more than a quarter of a century to subjugate what is now Wales and the Marches. Clearly, the Celtic tribes put up fierce resistance and cannot have been negligible either in numbers or in any military sense.

By the mid 50s, gains on the Welsh borderland were consolidated with the establishment of legionary fortresses at Usk and Wroxeter. Total victory was almost in sight when, in AD 60, disaster struck. The rebellion raised by Boudicca, queen of the *Iceni* (from the area which is now Norfolk), not only postponed the conquest of Wales, but also proved a major set-back to the new province as a whole.

Under the Emperor Vespasian, a new governor, Julius Frontinus (AD 74-7), was charged with the task of finally subjugating the Welsh tribes. With Usk and Wroxeter evacuated, legionary bases were constructed at Caerleon and Chester. From these fortresses, Frontinus and his successor, Agricola, created a tight military network of about 36 auxiliary forts linked by an all-weather road system. The forts housed infantry and cavalry units, between 500 and 1,000 men, whose job it was to police the new territory. An uneasy peace ensued, a peace which was to last as the native tribes gradually accepted the benefits brought by Rome — the *pax Romana*.

The military installations were first built almost entirely of wood, the notable exception being the great Fortress Baths at Caerleon, which seems to have been constructed of stone and concrete from the outset. Elsewhere, it was only during the earlier 2nd century that stone replaced timber buildings. By this time, however, there must have been a fairly widespread acceptance of Roman rule, since by about AD 130 most of the Welsh auxiliary forts had been partially or totally abandoned. Brecon Gaer and *Segontium* are two of the few examples where 2nd-century stone buildings are known. Caerleon, on the other hand, was to remain the permanent base of the Second Augustan Legion (*Legio II Augusta*), where a number of phases of building and rebuilding in stone were undertaken. Today, the remains of the fortress — *Isca* — represent one of the most important Roman military sites in northern Europe.

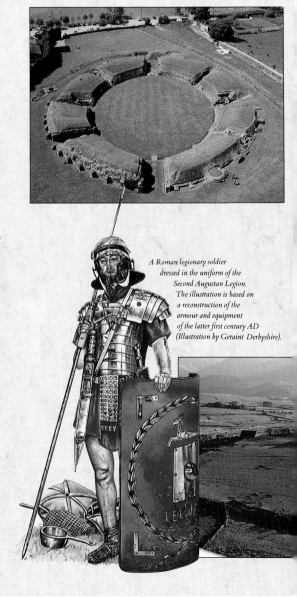

A Roman legionary soldier dressed in the uniform of the Second Augustan Legion. The illustration is based on a reconstruction of the armour and equipment of the latter first century AD (Illustration by Geraint Derbyshire).

Part of the walls of the Roman town of Caerwent. Romanization of civilian life followed the military conquest of Wales and Caerwent was established as the tribal capital of the Silures. The impressive stone walls stand up to 18 feet high.

One of the two circular stone huts at Din Lligwy, Anglesey. This is one of several stone buildings surrounded by a rectangular enclosure wall. It was probably built late during the Roman period and reflects a local interpretation of the Romanized way of rural life.

A coin of the usurper emperor, Magnus Maximus (By permission of the National Museum of Wales)

An aerial view of the Roman fort at Tomen y Mur, Gwynedd. This is one of a network of small forts established across Wales during the Roman occupation. It is interesting to note that a medieval castle mound or motte was later constructed within the earlier lines of the fort (Photography by Peter Humphries).

Following the military conquest, a degree of Romanization spread amongst the native population. In Wales the archaeological evidence, especially from the southeast, shows many of the trappings associated with the Roman world. By the end of the 1st century a tribal capital had been established at Caerwent, *Venta Silurum* — the market town of the *Silures*. Eventually, this settlement had its 'town hall', public baths, temples, and large courtyard houses, complete with mosaics and underfloor heating. In the west, too, evidence for a further tribal capital has been uncovered by archaeologists at Carmarthen — *Moridunum* — where the remains of an amphitheatre can be seen outside the modern town. Not far away, at Dolau Cothi, the Roman gold mines show how trade and industry were fostered.

Again, in the south-east, there is evidence for substantial villa-style farms, notably at Llantwit Major, and at Ely and Llandough on the outskirts of Cardiff. In addition, many lesser farmsteads reveal conspicuous signs of Romanization in this area. Elsewhere in Wales, rural settlements seem to demonstrate closer links with late prehistoric traditions. Single family homesteads were scattered in most parts, some showing signs of defence and a level of integration within the Roman economy. In the northwest, for instance, these homesteads were often stone constructions, with a variety of circular and rectangular buildings, as at Din Lligwy in Anglesey.

There is much evidence to attest that from the later 3rd century, the west coast of Wales was subject to increasing threat from Irish raiders — just one element in the mounting pressure around the borders of the empire. A system of coastal installations and strongpoints was raised around the southeast coast of England, and there is now much evidence for a network of defences in Wales. A new fort was built at Cardiff; and a small fortlet at Caer Gybi, Holyhead, probably dates to this time. Other forts appear to have existed at Loughor and Neath, and similar claims have been made for Pembroke.

The 4th century was a period of general insecurity throughout the province as a whole, and the military presence in Wales was severely depleted when the usurper, Magnus Maximus, left Britain for the Continent in the 380s. An official Roman presence ceased around 410, when the central government instructed the towns of Britain to look to their own defence. However, the economic infrastructure on which the Roman way of life depended had long broken down. There was never any deliberate abandonment of Britain, but rather events on the Continent simply delayed a reassertion of central control until such time as there was no strictly Roman province left to recover. So it was that the settled society of the *pax Romana* in Wales gave way to something quite different.

EARLY MEDIEVAL WALES

*T*he period between Roman empire and Norman Conquest is one of quite exceptional obscurity, with few surviving monuments to provide tangible links.

The 5th and 6th centuries are often referred to as the 'age of saints', and much has been written on the spread of Christianity under the influence of the so-called 'Celtic saints' — tireless missionaries journeying along all the western seaways between Brittany, Cornwall, Wales and Ireland to spread this message. Though there undoubtedly remains an element of reality in this picture, studies by modern historians have begun to sound a note of caution. Some, for example, argue that the diffusion and influence of Christianity in late Roman Britain were far more deep-rooted than had once been thought. As such, the foundations for a 'Welsh Church' had already been laid. We must be careful, too, about assuming that the element *llan* in Welsh place-names indicates the site of an early church. *Llan* probably began by signifying a burial enclosure, then a cemetery with a church, then the church itself, and now by any superimposed village or even a town — like Llandudno. In the end, all that is certain is that it implies a continuous Christian locality, probably going back many centuries.

The situation is no less obscure when we turn to famous 'monastic' sites such as St Davids, or St Illtud's important foundation at Llantwit Major. Archaeologists are hard pressed to provide even the slightest information on the nature of the buildings there. Those seeking a clearer indication of Christian activity are on firmer ground when considering the various inscribed tombstones and crosses collectively known as early Christian monuments. Over 400 are recorded from all parts of Wales, with dates ranging from the 5th to the 11th centuries. Many have been moved, from their original locations, but occasionally they stand isolated, even in open ground. More often they can be seen in churchyards, or even built into the fabric of the church itself. Important local collections have been gathered at Margam, and in the parish church at Llantwit Major. The earliest examples are quite plain, and generally served as tombstones or grave-markers. Later monuments include the 'Samson Cross' at Llantwit, and the fine pillar crosses at Carew and Nevern, all of which are far more elaborate.

St David, the patron saint of Wales. This modern statue by Sir Goscombe John is in Cardiff City Hall (By courtesy of Cardiff City Council).

The decoration on this stone cross from Whitford, Clwyd is one of the few surviving indications of Viking influence in eleventh-century Wales.

The cathedral church of St Asaph. A religious site with origins extending back to AD 560 in the early Christian period.

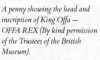

A penny showing the head and inscription of King Offa — OFFA REX (By kind permission of the Trustees of the British Museum).

Offa's Dyke, near Llangollen. Now a favourite trail with walkers, this eighth-century frontier built by the king of Mercia was once a formidable barrier controlling the border between England and Wales.

A scene from the great Welsh law book pronouncing on the law relating to falconers and falcons. The laws went under the name of Hywel Dda (d. 949-50) — Howell the Good — since they contained a core of material brought together in his time. This illustration is from the celebrated mid thirteenth-century copy of the laws (By courtesy of the National Library of Wales, Peniarth Ms. 28, f.4r).

In the early post-Roman centuries, Wales was politically divided into smallish kingdoms lying around the central upland core of the country. We know of a few defensive sites such as Dinas Powys in South Glamorgan, or Deganwy and Dinas Emrys in Gwynedd, but it is not known to what extent these were typical settlements. From this rather dim background emerges Arthur, famed in legend, the warrior king and foremost hero of the ancient British, who is said to have won a number of famous victories and held back the advance of the Anglo Saxons for a generation.

By the latter half of the 8th century, Offa, ruler of the Midland kingdom of Mercia, had built the famous dyke which bears his name. It was much the longest as well as the most striking man-made boundary in the whole of medieval western Europe, and clearly came to play an important role in shaping the perception of the extent and identity of Wales.

From the 9th to the 11th centuries a threatening cloud lowered sombrely over Welsh and Saxon alike, in the shape of the Vikings — insatiable in their lust for adventure, battle, and the spoils of war. The shores of Britain were terrorized by these warriors, who plundered not only the coastline but deep inland, disrupting entire communities. Some success was achieved against these raiders by Rhodri Mawr (Rhodri the Great), ruler of Gwynedd, who won a victory over the Danish in 856 but was eventually forced into exile in Ireland. It is surprising, therefore, that, despite their undoubted influence, apart from place-names (such as Bardsey, Fishguard, Milford, Skomer, Swansea), the Vikings have left little in the way of monuments in the landscape. Indeed, perhaps the most notable signs are those upon the style of decoration used on the great crosses of the 10th and 11th centuries, like those at Carew and Maen Achwyfan at Whitford.

The unity established by Rhodri Mawr in the 9th century was to prove short-lived. Aggravated by Anglo-Saxon intervention and the Viking raids, the country remained politically feeble and divided. Again, although his laws long outlived his death, the cohesiveness brought about by Hywel Dda (Howell the Good) was too fragile to extend beyond the reign in which it was achieved.

One last powerful ruler managed to bring a measure of unity before the Norman Conquest. Gruffudd ap Llywelyn, from his initial seizure of power in Gwynedd in 1039, became the dominant figure in Wales. During the last eight years of his life (1055-63), he held the whole country under his sway; a position founded on military might and personal dependence. Once again, though, his downfall and death left a vacuum of authority and strength. Within a decade, the Welsh were facing a new and very real threat, more powerful than anything they had ever faced before — the Normans.

THE NORMAN CONQUEST AND EARLY CASTLES

An imaginative drawing of an attack on a motte and bailey castle. It was the Normans who introduced castles to Wales, and they were soon taken up by the Welsh princes. Many hundreds of these earth and timber fortifications were rapidly established across the country (Illustration by Terry Ball).

A scene from the Bayeux tapestry, showing heavily armed Norman knights.

The Norman barons responsible for the conquest of Wales were a small group of men, rarely exceeding twenty in number who, in the immediate aftermath of Hastings, were far too busy with the problems of security and control in England and in Normandy itself to give much attention to Wales. However, the defence of a frontier soon turned to aggressive expansion. As a contemporary historian recorded, the Normans were 'a warlike race ... moved by fierce ambition to lord it over others'. Having practised the techniques in England and elsewhere, they well understood that the first rule of successful appropriation was to make sure of the territories overrun. To this end, the Normans had developed the castle.

Castles had not existed anywhere in Wales before the Norman Conquest. Yet over the following two centuries many hundreds were to be established. In order to understand the pattern of building a little more clearly, it is as well to think from the outset of a three-fold division.

First, by far the largest group of castles were those built by the Anglo–Norman lords of the March (from the French word *marche* meaning 'frontier'). The Marcher lordships eventually swung in a great arc from Chester in the north to Chepstow in the south, and then west to Pembroke. The grandest and most powerful of these strongholds were those built by the lords themselves: Caerphilly, Cardiff, Chepstow, Kidwelly, and the rest. But there were smaller examples, too, such as Bronllys and Tretower, built by followers and lieutenants of the major barons.

The second group was confined largely to the north and west of the country, the area known from the late 12th century as *pura Wallia* (pure Wales). Following the Norman Conquest, it was to take 200 years before Edward I extended the overlordship of the English kings to this area. The Welsh princes had, however, begun to imitate the Norman example soon after 1100, and gradually castles spread throughout their territories. Today, fine later Welsh stone building can be seen at Dinas Brân, Dinefwr, Dolbadarn, or Dolwyddelan.

The stone keep at Cardiff Castle atop a lofty mound still surrounded by a moat. Traditionally, the castle was begun in about 1093 by Robert fitz Hamon, during the Norman conquest of Glamorgan. Recent work has suggested that the motte may have been raised by William the Conqueror himself, about 1081.

Dolbadarn Castle, Gwynedd – a castle of the Welsh princes.

A view along the western curtain wall of White Castle where a substantial moat still survives. Although begun in the early Norman period, White Castle was in royal hands by the late twelfth century when further building work appears to have been commissioned by Henry II.

A further section from the Bayeux tapestry, this time showing how the Normans consolidated their victory at Hastings by constructing a castle.

Finally, in the background of this castle-building in Wales stalk the figures of the English kings. Until the late 13th century, their influence and involvement were not great, but, when employed, the royal hand was generally steady and the policy assured. Though having something of a chequered history, Carmarthen served as a royal castle from the reign of King Henry I (1100-35). At Newcastle, Bridgend, and White Castle, substantial building works in the 1180s were probably commissioned by Henry II. All of this, of course, was eventually overshadowed by the enormous programme of construction undertaken by Edward I between 1276 and 1296. In organizational and architectural skill, the breathtaking achievements of this period far surpassed anything hitherto attempted in the British Isles.

Having grasped this threefold division, the spread and development of castles across the Welsh landscape offer the traveller their own story. It begins in the immediate wake of the initial Norman advance. Plundering ruthlessly along the river valleys and coastal plains, the Norman lords set out to terrorize the country and force the Welsh into subjection. As early as 1067 William the Conqueror placed William fitz Osbern, one of his most trusted confidants, at Hereford. By 1071 Roger of Montgomery had been installed at Shrewsbury, and Hugh of Avranches ('the Fat') at Chester. In each case a new earldom was created, and in each case the new earl was granted royal demesne in the county and control of the county town. Within these virtually independent lordships — the foundation of the March itself — the earls ruled as miniature kings.

Before his death in 1071, fitz Osbern had overrun much of south-east Wales, and his exploits had set the pattern for the remaining conquest of this area. Earl Roger thrust up the valley of the Severn and established his main base at Montgomery. In the north, meanwhile, Hugh the Fat entrusted the task of pushing forward along the coast to his ambitious cousin, Robert of Rhuddlan, so called after the castle he had built on the Clwyd by 1073. Following Robert's death, probably in 1093, Earl Hugh maintained the advance by holding castles as far forward as Caernarfon and Aberllleiniog on Anglesey.

Following the death of the Welsh ruler, Rhys ap Tewdwr, in 1093, the invaders crashed into the south west from all sides. In addition, near Carmarthen William fitz Baldwin, sheriff of Devon, made conquests in the king's name. The de Braose family moved into Radnor, Bernard of Neufmarché completed his conquest of Brecon, and

Glamorgan was quickly and firmly overrun by Robert fitz Hamon.

In all of these initial advances, the castle was the means by which short-term victory was converted into conquest and domination. Almost without exception, these early examples were constructed of earth and timber (see p. 110). They could be thrown up rapidly — often by forced labour — and were to prove infinitely adaptable. Nor should we underestimate their role as symbols of the new ruling power. Mounds towering up to 40 ft high, surmounted with timberwork and bedecked with shields and other decorations, were meant to overawe the Welsh as much as Edward I's fortresses in a later age. It is difficult to envisage the overall effect now, but sturdy mottes can still be seen at Twthill in Rhuddlan, and below later stone buildings at Cardiff and Grosmont.

Only in the most securely held areas of the March do we find substantial stone castles of early date. The outstanding example is the work of William fitz Osbern at Chepstow, where the keep — still the core of the castle today — was built during 1067-71, and was quite exceptional for the period. Gradually, as the 12th century progressed, the use of stone became more common, sometimes at new sites, but more often replacing earlier timber constructions. Ogmore is one instance where a hefty masonry keep was raised at this time, and there is also 12th-century work at neighbouring Coity and Newcastle, Bridgend. The shell-keeps at Cardiff and Tretower, the great tower at Monmouth, and the initial keep at White Castle were again completed well before 1200.

During the long reign of King Henry II (1154-89) a kind of uneasy peace gradually emerged. By about 1165 the Anglo-Norman advance in Wales seemed to be faltering, with the barons of the south-west turning to Ireland in search of easier gains. The king caught the mood of change, and with great statecraft began negotiating agreements with Welsh princes. The native rulers met Henry half-way, recognizing him as overlord, and in return they were given virtual freedom to rule their own lands. So it was that Owain Gwynedd (1137-70) was able to build up his power base in the north-west. Even more dramatic was the rise and success of Deheubarth in the south-west under Rhys ap Gruffudd — the Lord Rhys as the king called him.

The end of Henry II's reign marks something of a watershed. It would be some years before an English king would invade Wales again. What is more, the map of the division of the country between Marcher lordships and Welsh principalities had reached the shape that was to last, in the main, right through to 1277 and the conquests of Edward I.

A silver penny of Henry I (1100-35) minted at Cardiff. The presence of a mint suggests that south-east Wales, at least, was securely held by the Normans at this time (By permission of the National Museum of Wales).

Chepstow Castle was one of the first Norman castles in Britain to be constructed in stone, probably between 1067-71. Here the castle is seen from the east, looking over the outer gatehouse towards the Great Tower.

Although Tretower was never as substantial as Chepstow Castle, the stone shell keep was probably completed in the twelfth century. The great round tower, seen here rising out of the ruins of its predecessor, was added in the early thirteenth century.

King Henry II, who reached agreements with both Marcher lords and native Welsh princes during his long and illustrious reign, is seen here seated in this twelfth-century manuscript (By courtesy of the National Library of Ireland, Ms. 700).

A carved stone head, possibly of Llywelyn ab Iorwerth, found at Deganwy Castle (By permission of the National Museum of Wales).

The round tower at Skenfrith Castle, built by the influential Marcher lord, Hubert de Burgh.

DEVELOPMENTS IN THE 13TH CENTURY

*T*he course of political developments and resultant castle–building in Wales in the 13th century can be charted mainly by reference to the achievements of two gifted rulers: Llywelyn ab Iorwerth ('the Great', 1173-1240) and his grandson, Llywelyn ap Gruffudd ('the Last', who was killed in 1282).

By 1201 Llywelyn the Great had gained supremacy of Gwynedd, and further advanced his position in 1205 by marrying Joan, the illegitimate daughter of King John. As his influence extended to the whole of native Wales, the goodwill of the crown quickly turned to outright hostility. But despite John's devastating campaign of 1211 in north Wales, Llywelyn's power base remained intact. Indeed, his sweeping advances into the southern Marches in 1215 struck deep at the heart of baronial control in these areas. It was soon clear, to both king and Marcher lord alike, that serious defences were needed if the Welsh were to be held in check.

Two of the most influential southern lords — William Marshall, earl of Pembroke, and Hubert de Burgh, earl of Kent — had already introduced major new initiatives into castle design. In particular, the appearance of round towers owes much to their experience of warfare and castle development in France. Marshall's Pembroke and de Burgh's Skenfrith, for example, were models for many others in the southern March. They were models, too, for defence against the growing strength of the Welsh prince.

The first marked offensive against Llywelyn was in fact launched by Marshall's son, William Marshall the younger. In 1223, with a considerable army brought over from Ireland, he retook the castles at Carmarthen and Cardigan and began building the massive main defences at Cilgerran. Later in the same year, the young Henry III and his minister Hubert de Burgh led an army to Montgomery and began the powerful castle on the rock there. The work at both sites was extremely formidable, and in many ways characteristic of the strongholds of the 13th century yet to come. Mighty curtain walls flanked by big round towers were to become the order of the day. At this time, de Burgh's Grosmont and the king's Painscastle were other important additions to the stock of masonry castles on the frontiers of Wales.

The tomb effigy of William Marshall, earl of Pembroke, at the Temple Church in the City of London.

Meanwhile, Llywelyn the Great was busy building his own stone castles within the territories he controlled. Castell y Bere and Ewloe, for instance, bear distinct hallmarks of his technique. In contrast, the gatehouse at Criccieth and the round tower at Dolbadarn are clear indications of Llywelyn's experience of Anglo-Norman constructions.

Following Llywelyn's death in 1240, his sons were soon engaged in power struggles in Gwynedd. It was not until his grandson, Llywelyn ap Gruffudd, emerged as sole ruler in 1255 that native Wales had once more found a leader. In this role, Llywelyn the Last quickly showed his true metal, and by 1258 he had received oaths of homage and allegiance from virtually all the Welsh princes. He went on to exploit the difficulties encountered by Henry III during the civil war with his barons (1264–65), led by Simon de Montfort. Exhausted by this continuing political dissension in both England and Wales, the king was forced to acknowledge Llywelyn's proud title as prince of Wales by the Treaty of Montgomery of 1267.

In the March, the response to this new and overbearing threat was somewhat predictable. Llywelyn and his allies had made considerable inroads into the lordships of the south and had managed to take a number of lesser castles. Behind the borders, however, the great stone Marcher strongholds were holding like sheet-anchors, and there was now further incentive to add to their stock. Foremost among the new building of this time was that begun at Caerphilly by Gilbert de Clare in 1268. Situated in the northern hill territory of the lordship of Glamorgan, it was attacked and destroyed by Llywelyn in 1270. It was retaken by de Clare, and the castle subsequently built was to prove the culmination of military construction to date. Elsewhere, the impressive walls-within-walls principle seen at Caerphilly was also taken up by Payn de Chaworth at Kidwelly. White Castle, too, was heavily refortified by the king's agents in the 1260s or 1270s.

Llywelyn himself was busy strengthening his grandfather's castles at Criccieth, Ewloe, and Dolwyddelan. Moreover, in 1273 he started to build a new castle at Dolforwyn, high above the Severn valley, posing a challenge to the royal frontier post at Montgomery. The prince's refusal to abandon this project was just one incident in an eventual catalogue of disagreements with the new king of England, Edward I (1272–1307).

Llywelyn ab Iorwerth's great gatehouse at Criccieth Castle. Probably built around 1230-40, it may well have been modelled on a similar gatehouse at Beeston Castle, Cheshire.

Caerphilly Castle, which lay in the Marcher lordship of Glamorgan. It was built by Gilbert de Clare, largely in response to the threats posed by Llywelyn ap Gruffudd's southern incursions.

Dolforwyn Castle, Powys — the only castle entirely built by Llywelyn ap Gruffudd.

THE CASTLES OF KING EDWARD I

Caernarfon, Conwy and Harlech — three of the magnificent military fortresses built by King Edward I in his determined efforts to subdue the Welsh. These castles, together with Beaumaris have been justly recognized as masterpieces of medieval military architecture and accordingly been given World Heritage Site status.

A fifteenth-century French manuscript illustration showing the use of helicoidal (spiral) scaffolding in the building of round towers. This method of construction was used in a number of King Edward I's castles in north Wales (By kind permission of the British Library, Royal Ms. 15 D III, f. 15v).

*F*rom the outset, Llywelyn seemed almost to go out of his way to court Edward's anger. In particular, he refused to yield the homage and money payments owing to the king under the terms of the Treaty of Montgomery. He tempted fate yet further by arranging to marry Eleanor, daughter of the rebel baron Simon de Montfort, an act destined to strain Edward's patience to the limit.

Enough was enough, and by 1276-77 Edward had decided to settle accounts with the recalcitrant Welsh prince. The king created three military commands based on Chester, Montgomery, and Carmarthen, a plan aimed at driving the Welsh back into the Gwynedd heartlands. Edward himself took the field at Chester in July 1277, and by August he had some 15,600 troops in his pay. Llywelyn was thus confronted with vastly superior odds. Cut off by the English fleet from his corn supplies in Anglesey, he had no choice but to sue for peace. The Treaty of Aberconwy represented a comprehensive humiliation for the prince of Wales. Stripped of the overlordship he had won ten years earlier, Llywelyn was also deprived of most of the territory he had gained outside Gwynedd.

In this huge operation, the king had demonstrated that he had the might to organize and deploy forces on a scale unprecedented in the history of warfare in medieval Britain. Moreover, from the very beginning, Edward was determined to ensure the military permanence of his initial success in Wales. To this end the stone castle was to occupy a cardinal role. The whole strategy of foundation was clearly thought out by the king and his advisors in advance. Little use was made, for example, of his father's great northern castles at Deganwy and Dyserth. Instead, four new royal castles were begun with great speed, at Aberystwyth, Builth, Flint, and Rhuddlan. The king's hand and resources were also involved in at least three other constructions, at Hawarden, Hope (Caergwrle), and Ruthin.

As the walls of these new strongholds began to rise in the landscape, King Edward set about consolidating his political and administrative position in Wales. On the frontiers of the March and in certain older key castles he placed trusted English officials, willing lieutenants who soon extended their legal authority aggressively over the surrounding countryside.

In defeat, Llywelyn showed restraint, not so his brother, Dafydd, and other Welsh rulers, who rose in co-ordinated revolt in March 1282. They quickly took the castles of Hawarden and Aberystwyth, and were poised to set all Wales aflame. Llywelyn, for his part, true to all his instincts and previous experience, joined the revolt and placed himself at the head of his people's cause.

The king was outraged and moved with all speed to prevent the revolt spreading. Again he established three commands in west, mid, and north Wales, squeezing the Welsh back into Snowdonia. Llywelyn, determined to avoid a repeat of 1277, broke out to the south, possibly in an attempt to take Builth Castle. In December 1282 he was killed a few miles from Builth, in or after a major skirmish with a larger Marcher force. Not only the prince of Wales, but the hopes for an independent Welsh state had finally been crushed by the awesome determination of King Edward I.

In a programme of work even more breathtaking than that begun in 1277, three more significant royal castles were begun at Caernarfon, Conwy, and Harlech, inspired by the genius of Master James of St George (see Page 38). Edward further underpinned his plan by repairing the earlier Welsh castles at Castell y Bere, Criccieth, and Dolwyddelan, whilst persuading trusted Marcher lords to build their own fortresses at Denbigh, Holt, and Chirk. Ten years later, following a dangerous uprising of 1294-95 led by Madog ap Llywelyn, Edward commissioned one further castle at Beaumaris on the Isle of Anglesey. Begun in April 1295, this was to prove the ultimate in medieval military architecture, perhaps the most perfectly planned castle in the entire British Isles. Together, this resulting chain of powerful castles acted as a strait-jacket, ensuring the final and total submission of *pura Wallia* — pure Wales.

Dazzling though their design and construction were, it is important to see Edward I's castles in context. Individually, they could be matched and even exceeded by great contemporary baronial strongholds such as Gilbert de Clare's Caerphilly. Their significance rests in their quality as a group. Constructed at break-neck speed, and financed by unparalleled investment, they were the concerted focus of the most up-to-date European thinking in castle planning. Against de Clare's Caerphilly or Roger Bigod's Chepstow, Edward I could set up to ten immense fortresses of his own.

Edward's reward for this huge investment was lasting peace and security. The English Marcher lords and the Crown remained free from Welsh threat and revolt for the next century. Gradually, for the Welsh, the full extent of the catastrophe became an overbearing reality. As a later poet was to put it, the country was now to be ruled and controlled under 'the tower of the bold conqueror'.

Llywelyn ab Iorwerth's castle at Dolwyddelan, Gwynedd. It controlled a principal routeway through Snowdonia, and its capture by Edward I in 1283 was of immense strategic importance in the English conquest of Gwynedd.

Edward I successfully persuaded Henry de Lacy, earl of Lincoln to build Denbigh Castle to strengthen the royal chain of castles in north Wales.

Following the revolt of Madog ap Llywelyn in 1294-95, Edward I commissioned one last castle at Beaumaris, Anglesey. It is perhaps the most perfectly planned castle in the British Isles, displaying the ultimate development in medieval military architecture.

Edward of Caernarfon (later Edward II) created the first English Prince of Wales by his father King Edward I in 1301 (By permission of the British Library, Cotton Ms. Nero D II, f. 191v).

MEDIEVAL CATHEDRALS AND MONASTERIES OF WALES

Penmon

St Asaph
Abercorwy
Bangor
Beddgelert
Ruthin
Valle Crucis

Bardsey
Cymer
Strata Marcella
Llanllyon

Cwmhir
Strata Florida
Llanllyr

Cardigan
St Dogmaels
Talley
Llanthony

St Davids
Whitland
Carmarthen
Grace Dieu
Haverfordwest
St Clears
Abergavenny
Monmouth
Pill
Kidwelly
Tintern
Pembroke
Usk
St Kynemark
Caldey
Neath
Llantarnam
Chepstow
Llangenydd
Margam
Malpas
Goldcliff
Llandaff
Ewenny
Cardiff

Basingwerk

† Cathedral Church
■ Benedictine, Cluniac, Tironian (Monks)
□ Cistercian (Monks)
◆ Augustinian, Premonstratensian (Regular Canons)
○ Nuns
–·– Diocesan Boundaries

St Davids bishop's palace and cathedral – a religious centre since the sixth century – it was substantially enlarged by Norman and later bishops, reflecting the power and wealth of the medieval church.

MONASTIC HOUSES AND CATHEDRAL CHURCHES

Dominant though the position of the castle was to become in the medieval Welsh landscape, we should not overlook those other major monuments introduced at this time, namely those associated with developments in the Church. Strange as it might seem, the new Norman ruling classes often combined the most ruthless butchery with acts of the most conventional piety. From the outset, however, a great deal of down-to-earth practicality underlay much of their ecclesiastical reform and patronage. Foremost among the symbols of Norman ideals for the Church were diocesan reorganization and the spread of the monastic orders.

To the Normans, familiar with mainstream developments in Latin Christendom on the Continent, the Welsh church must have presented a bizarre medley of archaic customs, institutions, and practices. They sought to impose their own authority on the church in Wales, seeing it as much as a religious duty as a political necessity. As in England, the most obvious way to ensure such authority was in the appointment and control of bishops. By 1127 new prelates at Bangor, Llandaff, and St Davids had acknowledged the supremacy of Canterbury, and in 1143 the head of the newly created or recreated See of St Asaph followed suit. This time, too, saw the clear demarcation of the territories and boundaries of the four dioceses, the configurations of which were to be retained until this century.

Even in England, where the Anglo-Saxons had a greater tradition of stone church building, the Norman prelates often swept all aside and set about raising impressive new cathedrals. In Wales they soon arranged for tremendous bursts of building activity. Bishop David at Bangor, Urban at Llandaff, and Bernard at St Davids began work in the early 12th century. At St Davids, however, Bernard's church was destroyed by fire in 1182, and it was Bishop Peter de Leia (1176-98) who was responsible for the striking work seen in the nave today. At Llandaff, progress with the nave was slow, and it was only gradually completed, in the new Gothic style, towards the end of the 12th century. This early Gothic influence had spread westwards via the great churches at Glastonbury and Wells in Somerset, and at Llandaff its finest expression is seen in the early 13th-century west front.

We know little of the early cathedrals at Bangor and St Asaph, since they were severely damaged during the Welsh wars of King Edward I. Both buildings now date largely from the later Middle Ages.

Medieval bishops accommodated themselves in residences seen by them as commensurate with their status as princes of the Church. At Llandaff, for example, an impressive gatehouse to the bishop's palace still survives. But it is at St Davids, amid a group of medieval buildings unsurpassed in Wales, that we gain an insight into the true aspirations of these mighty prelates. Few Welsh landowners were greater or wealthier than the bishops of St Davids, and a succession of builders among them expressed this wealth in constructing the magnificent palace which survives in the cathedral precinct. Moreover, at St Davids, these bishops were Marcher lords in their own right, with vast estates throughout the diocese. Associated with these estates, a further comfortable palace was built at Lamphey, and at Llawhaden a small but powerful little castle stood at the centre of another group of rich possessions.

The Normans also used the monastic orders to strengthen their control over the Church in the early conquest years (see p. 120). Gradually, however, as the 12th century progressed, the Cistercians in particular took firm root in 'pure Wales' and were warmly supported and patronized by the Welsh princes.

The legacy of monastic building in Wales is considerable, and much the most important sites are covered in the gazetteer. As with castles, the earliest constructions were of wood, but the religious orders were to initiate many varied, and often extensive, building programmes right through to the Dissolution of the Monasteries, 1536–40. In the security of the March, sombre stone churches in the Norman Romanesque style began to rise in the 12th century, with fine examples still to be seen at Ewenny, Margam, and at Chepstow where the Benedictine priory church now serves parish needs. Such early churches, as well as their accompanying domestic buildings, may have proved sufficient for the fledgeling communities, but with growth and success came demands for larger and more impressive buildings.

The late 12th and 13th centuries may be regarded as the high point of monastic building in Wales. The period begins with the grace and refinement of the churches at Llanthony, Strata Florida and Talley. It continues, for example, with the breathtaking elegance of the early 13th-century chapter house at Margam, and concludes with the immense new churches at Tintern and Neath — though work at the latter continued into the 14th century.

Essentially, in Wales as elsewhere, the buildings in a medieval monastery were laid out in a fairly distinct and somewhat standard plan, which was practical and made the best possible use of natural light. This plan was composed of three main elements. The most important of these was the church, the focus of the spiritual and physical life of the

The impressive Norman south doorway of Llandaff Cathedral

Detail above the west doorway at Llandaff Cathedral.

The spectacular ruins of Tintern Abbey have pleased scholars and tourists alike for more than two centuries. This view within the great abbey church was painted by J M W Turner sometime during the 1790s, when Tintern was at the height of its 'romantic' appeal.

PLAN SHOWING THE LAYOUT OF A MEDIEVAL MONASTERY

Neath Abbey was one of the larger monasteries of medieval Wales. At the Dissolution of 1536-40 it was converted to a country house.

The Cistercian abbey of Cymer was one of the monasteries patronized by the native princes of Wales.

monastery. It was generally orientated east-west, and was nearly always cruciform (cross) in shape. The choir and presbytery — with the high altar — were located at the east, with the nave at the west end. The two arms of the cross were formed by transepts. The nucleus of the monastic plan, however, was the cloister, a broad passage or gallery surrounding an open rectangular space and giving direct access to those buildings in which the community lived, administered business, cared for their sick and old, and provided hospitality for guests. It was the cloister which gave its peculiar character to the entire complex, and became in time a synonym for the monastic house itself and for the life lived within.

The cloister was usually located on the south side of the church, again to take advantage of shelter and light. Occasionally, as at Tintern, for reasons of water supply or other physical conditions, it was reluctantly placed to the north. Around the open rectangle, although the precise arrangement of rooms might vary slightly from one order to another, the overall pattern remained remarkably uniform. The east range included the chapter house (an important room where the monks met each day to hear a chapter of their *rule* read and to discuss the business of the house), the main latrine, and the monks' dormitory on the first floor. Next, the range opposite the church — generally on the south — was occupied by the dining hall of the monks, with perhaps the kitchen at one end. Finally, in Benedictine houses, the basement of the west range often served as a store, with guest accommodation or the superior's lodging on the first floor. In contrast, at Cistercian houses, this western range was given over to lay brothers for their dining hall and dormitory above.

The third element in the monastic plan was made up of those structures serving the daily needs of the monastery at large, and also providing facilities for the exploitation of outlying estates. These would have included barns, stables, a brewhouse, mill, dairy and so on, and were normally located in an area adjacent to the church and cloister known as the outer court.

Alas, few sites have complete layouts for us to observe today, but very full plans can be distinguished at Neath and Tintern. Elsewhere, one or other section of the monastery lies exposed, and it is not too difficult for us to envisage the disposition of the remaining buildings. At Cwmhir, Cymer, Llanthony, Strata Florida, and Talley, for example, it is the church which survives best. At Basingwerk and St Dogmaels there are interesting sections of the cloister buildings, and at the Augustinian priory of Haverfordwest archaeological excavations are gradually uncovering a fairly extensive arrangement of both church and cloister.

LATER MEDIEVAL CASTLES

The 'fortified manor house' at Weobley exemplifies the transition from castle towards domestic residence in the later Middle Ages. This reconstruction drawing shows the castle as it may have appeared about 1500 (Illustration by Terry Ball).

A gilt-bronze harness mounting, bearing the arms of Owain Glyndŵr, found at Harlech. Glyndŵr held the castle at Harlech for four years from 1404-08 (By permission of the National Library of Wales).

Raglan Castle seen from the air — one of the most glorious castles of fifteenth-century chivalry.

After the final conquest by King Edward I, the apparent need for castles quickly diminished. New works, it is true, continued into the 14th century, but very often there was a marked change in character. The transition from military stronghold to comfortable residence was in many cases already under way, a change reflected in the 'fortified manor house' at Weobley, for instance.

For much of the 14th century peace was maintained until the charismatic Owain Glyndŵr rose in revolt and was proclaimed prince of Wales. At the height of the uprising, around 1400, it was only the strength of the stone network of castles which stood between Glyndŵr and the total overthrow of English power in Wales.

The continued importance of stone castles is emphasized by their usefulness to Glyndŵr himself. His two greatest prizes were Aberystwyth and Harlech which fell into his hands in 1404 and were held for four years. In possession of these major strongholds he was no longer merely the leader of an insurrection, he was a sovereign prince and effective ruler of large parts of western Wales. Harlech was eventually retaken at the end of 1408, or early in 1409, by Harry of Monmouth — the future King Henry V. As for the revolt, it was not effectively crushed, but rather, just petered out, Glyndŵr simply disappearing from the records in 1415.

In the half century after the Glyndŵr rebellion, Wales was in a state of uneasy calm. With the outbreak of civil war in 1455 — the Wars of the Roses — the castle had still not lost its place. Indeed, it was this situation in south-east Wales which gave rise to one of the most glorious and chivalrous castles of the 15th century — Raglan. Nothing short of exotic in the context of Wales, Raglan was built very much in the contemporary French manner, as was the new octagon tower at Cardiff Castle. Raglan was later transformed into a veritable palace, and reflects the meteoric rise to power of Sir William Herbert, under his patron Edward IV. Sir Roger Vaughan, was another who grasped his chances at this time with both hands, his building work at Tretower reflecting new wealth and influence, born from a troubled and war-torn country.

Sir William Herbert transformed Raglan into a veritable palace. In this manuscript illustration of about 1461–62, he is seen with his wife, Anne, kneeling at the feet of King Edward IV (By permission of the British Library, Royal Ms. 18 D II, f.6).

THE ARRIVAL OF THE COUNTRY HOUSE

William Somerset, third earl of Worcester, who brought Raglan up to the standards required by an Elizabethan gentleman (By courtesy of his grace the duke of Beaufort).

Oxwich 'Castle' on the Gower peninsula — a superb Elizabethan great house built by the Mansel family.

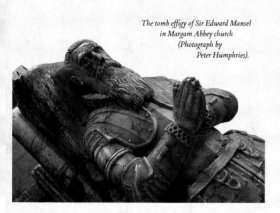

The tomb effigy of Sir Edward Mansel in Margam Abbey church (Photograph by Peter Humphries).

The Wars of the Roses were brought to an end at the battle of Bosworth in 1485. The accession of Henry VII, and the settled conditions fostered by the new Tudor dynasty, led to a more peaceful and orderly society, in which the need for castles as military strongholds had greatly diminished. The 16th century was also a period of remarkable economic growth and a prosperous countryside, all of which is reflected in outstanding architectural developments, particularly the arrival of the true country house. To begin with, though, the character of many of the great gentry houses of the 16th century continued to be influenced by medieval precedents. Some of the most prominent Elizabethan works represent large-scale transformations of earlier strongholds.

Foremost among those to take advantage of the new age were the Somersets, earls of Worcester, the leading aristocratic family in Wales at this time. It was the third earl (1549-89) who remodelled the hall and began the splendid long gallery at Raglan Castle. Further west, similar work was underway at Carew and Laugharne castles, where Sir John Perrot was busy refashioning them into palatial country mansions in the 1580s. At Oxwich, on the Gower peninsula, a house begun by Sir Rice Mansel was greatly enlarged by his son, Sir Edward, around 1559-80. In the north of the country, the Herbert family bought Powis Castle in 1587, and they began the long process of turning it into one of the grandest stately homes in Wales.

In contrast to the reshaping of medieval castles, the Dissolution of the Monasteries (1536-40) provided the financial wherewithal, as well as a convenient source of building material, for impressive Tudor country houses. At Ewenny, for example, the Carne family converted the monastic buildings into a comfortable residence. Yet more impressive is the mansion which was raised over the south-east corner of the former monastic cloister at Neath. The late medieval abbots had already begun a house in this area, and it may have been Sir Richard Williams who greatly extended this about 1560. Before the end of the century the house had passed to John Herbert, who may also have been responsible for some of the building work.

There were, however, the beginings of a much more radical influence on the development of gentry homes in the late 16th century. Slowly at first, the effects of the Renaissance — particularly the concern for more formal planning — began to take a firm hold on the builders and owners of great houses. One of the earliest examples revealing this new influence is

St Fagans Castle, with its symmetrical facades and high-pitched roofs, completed between 1560 and 1600. Nearby, at Beaupre, the superb Italianate porch was added to the Elizabethan mansion about 1600. In north Wales, Plas Mawr (1576-80), Conwy, again illustrates the early Renaissance trends. With the turn of the century came still greater breaks with tradition. Plas Teg, completed about 1610, and Ruperra Castle in Glamorgan, built in 1626, in many ways mark the arrival of the full Renaissance style to country houses in Wales.

THE CIVIL WAR

D espite the peaceful advances of the Tudor era, the castle as a military strongpoint was to have yet one last lease of life. When the Civil War broke out between the king and Parliament in 1642 Wales was almost wholly royalist, and a number of castles were garrisoned in Charles I's cause.

Conwy was renovated and refortified during 1642-43 by John Williams, archbishop of York, and was held for the king throughout the first Civil War. Caernarfon and Ruthin both withstood Parliamentarian sieges and raids during the first war, and only finally surrendered in 1646. Denbigh, too, was held for the king until the garrison was forced to abandon a hopeless struggle after a very long siege lasting from the end of 1645 through until October 1646. In the south-east, the staunch royalist marquess of Worcester held out at Raglan in the spring and summer of 1646, in one of the most hotly-contested sieges of the war. The marquess finally surrendered to Sir Thomas Fairfax on 19 August, long after the submission of the king and the collapse of his cause.

Pembroke Castle had been a firm Parliamentary base throughout this first war. In marked contrast, during the second war of 1648 it became a major royalist strongpoint. Cromwell himself arrived on 24 May to conduct the siege, but it was not until heavy cannon were brought by ship from Gloucester that he was able to achieve success. Several breaches were opened in the walls of the town and castle, pressing the king's men into submission in mid July.

Various other castles featured to a greater or lesser degree in these wars. Surprising as it may seem, though, cannon bombardment was not the principal cause for their destruction at the time. So powerfully constructed were the medieval stone defences, gunpowder was only part of the story. It was the subsequent 'slighting', ordered by Parliament, which caused the real damage.

Portrait of King Charles I, about 1645. Many Welsh castles saw action once again in support of the Royalist cause during the Civil War (By courtesy of the National Portrait Gallery).

Archbishop John Williams, who spent large sums of his own money in fortifying Conwy Castle for King Charles I (By courtesy of the Master and Fellows of St John's College, Cambridge).

Oliver Cromwell (By courtesy of the National Portrait Gallery).

The Great Tower at Raglan Castle — partially destroyed by Cromwell's demolition engineers, following its capture in 1646

Pembroke Castle — a major Royalist strongpoint during the second war of 1648.

FROM THE RESTORATION TO THE INDUSTRIAL ERA

The imposing facade of Erddig, built in the late seventeenth century.

The superb orangery at Margam built in 1787.

The iron master William Crawshay's 'baronial stronghold' at Cyfarthfa, Merthyr Tydfil.

The chapel Cardiff Castle (By courtesy of Cardiff City Council).

*A*fter the Restoration in 1660, developments in Renaissance building continued apace. Tredegar House, for example, was built about 1670, and is undoubtedly one of the most lavishly ornate of Welsh country houses. Smaller in scale, but no less impressive, is Great Castle House at Monmouth, constructed in 1673. Erddig, near Wrexham, is another late 17th-century great house laid out to a very formal plan about 1684-87.

New departures in the 18th century centred upon the refined elegance of the Georgian style. Nanteos, near Aberystwyth, was built in 1739, and also demonstrates the 18th-century trend towards flatter fronts in such houses, with the roof-line hidden behind a parapet. Later in the century, at Chirk, Richard Myddleton was busy transforming the border fortress built during the Welsh wars of King Edward I. Between 1763-73 magnificent state rooms with superb ceilings and a graceful entrance hall were built into the existing medieval stronghold. The Orangery erected at Margam in 1787 represents the buildings and taste of 18th-century landowners at their very finest.

From the end of the 18th century onwards, the Industrial Revolution completely changed the life of Wales. As industries such as coal, copper, iron, and slate boomed, vast fortunes were made by opportunist entrepreneurs. Encouraged by architects, some of these still saw the castle as the ultimate expression of wealth and status. So it was that the iron master William Crawshay commissioned Cyfarthfa Castle in 1825. The house overlooked his immensely successful ironworks, and in his way Crawshay was not so very far removed from the feudal magnates of a much earlier age. Later, between 1827 and 1840, Thomas Hopper designed a much more convincing 'Norman fortress' at Penrhyn Castle for the slate baron George Douglas-Pennant.

Such 19th-century developments were small-fry compared to the romantic extravagances yet to be lavished on two former medieval strongholds in south Wales. At Cardiff Castle and Castell Coch William Burges and the third marquess of Bute created the most remarkable mansions to be resurrected in the industrial age. With their lavish decoration, brimming with imagery, they have been seen as 'the ultimate in nostalgic escapism from the industrial squalor that everywhere accompanied the sources of wealth'.

Valle Crucis Abbey by J.M.W. Turner, 1775-1851 (By courtesy of the Trustees of the British Museum).

A GAZETTEER

OF CASTLES
& HISTORIC
PLACES
IN WALES

The following gazetteer is an alphabetical listing of almost 150 castles and other ancient and historic sites situated throughout Wales. It is not, of course, a comprehensive list. It concentrates on those monuments maintained by Cadw: Welsh Historic Monuments on behalf of the Secretary of State for Wales, together with those in the ownership of the National Trust. In each case, these sites are identified by the logo of the particular organization. The remaining sites are run and maintained by other bodies concerned with the built heritage of the country.

THE GAZETTEER

The essential attribute for inclusion in the gazetteer is that the monument is open to visitors at all reasonable hours, without prior appointment. Others have been chosen because of their historic significance, their interest to the visitor, or a combination of both.

The list includes a selection of prehistoric sites, including chambered tombs and hillforts. The Roman period is represented by the remains of both military and civilian settlements. Moving forward, the various inscribed and sculptured stones, known as early Christian monuments, are survivals from the centuries between the fall of Rome and the arrival of the Normans. Naturally enough, the gazetteer centres on the *stone* castles of the Middle Ages. Earthwork motte and bailey and ringwork sites are not listed (see p. 110). Other prominent medieval monuments include monastic remains and the cathedral churches. Parish churches, however, are beyond the scope of this volume, and these are not covered. The last major selection of sites includes the country houses and mansions from the post-medieval centuries.

ACCESS

Each entry has a map reference which locates the site in question on the appropriate 5 miles: 1 inch map, which appears on pp. 126-137. At the end of each individual site description, basic 'how to get there' information is also provided.

CHARGES

Entry to many sites is completely free. Entry fees, when applicable, vary from site to site. At the end of each individual entry, details are denoted by C (charge payable), or F (free access).

OPENING TIMES

The majority of F sites are open throughout the year at all reasonable hours. Most C sites are open at regular hours in the summer months; some, particularly those in the care of Cadw: Welsh Historic Monuments, are open throughout the year. The standard hours for the Cadw sites do vary, and specific opening times are not listed. It is recommended that visitors confirm these times beforehand (through local Tourist Information Centres or direct to Cadw: Welsh Historic Monuments — 0222 465511) to avoid disappointment.

Visitors on the Great Tower at Raglan Castle.

The picturesque timber-framed exterior of Aberconwy House, dating from the fourteenth century.

ABBEY CWMHIR, POWYS

Deep in the hills north of Llandrindod Wells stand the scant remains of a Cistercian monastery founded in 1176. Some traces of outside walls, bases of several nave piers and fragments of north and south transepts are all that remain of a large religious house, traditionally the burial place of Llywelyn, last of the Welsh native princes.

On minor road 5½m N of Llandrindod Wells. F.   *Ge2*

ABERCONWY HOUSE, CONWY, GWYNEDD

Aberconwy, a three-storeyed house with a picturesquely asymmetrical front, is one of Conwy's last remaining 14th-century timber-framed houses, and is in the ownership and care of The National Trust. The intricate leaded casement windows are of a later period. The ground floor is a National Trust shop. A noteworthy feature on the top floor is a 17th-century fireplace. Aberconwy houses the Conwy Exhibition, depicting the life of the borough from Roman to present times.

In town centre. C.   *Bb4*

ABERGAVENNY CASTLE, GWENT

Fragments are all that remain of a castle which once belonged to the notorious William de Braose, whose name became a by-word for treachery and cruelty in the Welsh Marches. Only the outer walls of two towers remain but part of a third tower is incorporated in the wall of the house standing at the foot of the castle mound. The remnants of the curtain walls probably date from the time of de Braose in the 12th century, but the castle's most substantial stonework is of the late 13th and 14th centuries. The great hall stretched from the polygonal tower to the gatehouse, its roof timbers springing from corbels which can still be seen high on the curtain wall.

The gatehouse was a late addition to the castle and may be a tribute to the strength of the Glyndŵr threat early in the 15th century. The castle stands in a pleasant park, just south of the town centre. A local museum is housed adjacent to the ruins.

S of town centre. F.   *Mc2*

Abergavenny Castle – the scene of twelfth-century treachery and mass murder.

ABERYSTWYTH CASTLE, DYFED

Aberystwyth's ruined towers stand on a windy headland above the seaside promenade, enjoying wide views of Cardigan Bay. The original Aberystwyth Castle was at or near Tanybwlch, on a hill above the Ystwyth, but the name was transferred to the present castle when building commenced there in 1277. This was one of Edward I's first castles in Wales, though it had nothing of the grandeur of Caernarfon or Conwy.

The castle was substantially completed by 1279, though a report by Bogo de Knovill, justiciar of west Wales, to Edward I in 1280 criticized the castle's construction: he states that the gate tower was 'shaken day in day out by the great crash of waves' through its foundation being placed too near the castle ditch. The castle has an unusual diamond plan, the idea being to block the rocky headland on which it stands: thus it had the sea on one side and a marsh on the other. The castle was taken by Owain Glyndŵr in 1404 but recaptured by Prince Henry, later Henry V. During the Civil War of

the 17th century, Thomas Bushell managed a mint there for King Charles.

A recent programme of clearance and archaeological excavation has revealed much of interest in the inner ward of the castle.

In public park on seafront. F.   Fe1

Bangor Cathedral, largely rebuilt after a fire which destroyed the eleventh-century church of Bishop David.

BANGOR CATHEDRAL, GWYNEDD

Bangor lays claim to being the oldest cathedral in Britain, and was originally founded about AD 525. The Normans, intent on the reorganization of the Welsh church, had refounded it by 1092. Between 1120-39, Bishop David built a stone cathedral, and it was here that Archbishop Baldwin and Gerald of Wales preached the Crusade in 1188. The building was badly damaged during the Welsh wars of King Edward I. The most prominent works in this little cathedral were completed between 1496 and 1534 in a simple Perpendicular style. The western tower, of about 1510-32, is almost parochial in character, but is well designed. The building was restored under Sir Gilbert Scott, 1866-75.

Though the interior is a little dark and gloomy, there is much of interest to be seen. The finest item is the 'Mostyn Christ', a superb wooden figure of about 1518

Aberystwyth Castle – one of the first castles to be built in Wales by King Edward I.

showing Christ at Calvary. It may have come from the dissolved Dominican friary at Rhuddlan. The arched tomb in the south transept may have been prepared for Bishop Anian I. In the nave, notice the 'dog tongs' used to remove unruly dogs from the church.

In the centre of Bangor. F.   Ae3

BARCLODIAD Y GAWRES BURIAL CHAMBER, RHOSNEIGR, ISLE OF ANGLESEY, GWYNEDD

Barclodiad y Gawres ('the Giantess's Apronful'), magnificently sited on the top of a cliff on the south-west coast of Anglesey, is one of the most interesting of all the Welsh Neolithic tombs. The site had been used mercilessly as a stone 'quarry' in the 18th century and was thought to hold little of value, until excavations in 1952-53 exposed one of the most exciting modern finds in a megalithic monument. Several stones in the passage and chambers were found to be decorated with a variety of incised lozenge, chevron, spiral and zig-zag patterns. Clearly of 'ritual' significance to the builders, such prehistoric rock art is best represented in the Boyne Valley passage graves of Ireland.

The mound of the tomb is restored, but copies the original and is some 90 ft in diameter. A 20 ft long passage leads into the central chambers. The cremated bones of two people were found in the undisturbed western chamber.

1½m SE of Rhosneigr on headland N of Porth Trecastell beach. F.   Ab3

BASINGWERK ABBEY, HOLYWELL, CLWYD

The chapter house at Basingwerk, where the monks met each day to hear read a chapter of their Rule.

The sad ruins of this abbey belie its glory in the days before the Dissolution of the Monasteries. Basingwerk was praised for the beauty of its setting and of its buildings in the 15th century. Guests, it seems, were so numerous by this time that they had to be accommodated for meals at two sittings, and had a choice of wines from France and Spain. All this, however, was a far cry from the early ideals of the monastic community here.

The abbey was founded about 1132 by Ranulf, earl of Chester, for an abbot and 12 monks of the French order of Savigny. In 1147 this order was absorbed by the Cistercians and Basingwerk eventually became subordinate to Buildwas Abbey in Shropshire. As with other Cistercian houses, its strict *Rule* and harsh life were severely compromised in the later Middle Ages.

Little remains of the 13th-century church, though the plan of its aisled nave, north and south transepts, and presbytery to the east are easily traced. Parts of the chapter house and novices' lodging, on the east side of the cloister,

belong to the 12th century. In the early 13th century the chapter house was extended. It was an important room, where the monks met each day to hear read a chapter of their *Rule*. Traces of the bench on which they sat can be seen around the walls. Further south in this eastern range, the room with the column bases was the warming house, the only place in the abbey where a fire was allowed. The monks' dining hall was rebuilt at right-angles to the southern range of the cloister in the later 13th century. Today, it is much the most impressive surviving room. Notice the remains of the hatch through which food was passed from the kitchen to the west.

Footpath from Greenfield village on A548, 1m NE of Holywell. F. Ca4

The Cistercian abbey of Basingwerk founded by Ranulf, earl of Chester in 1132.

Beaumaris Castle, Isle of Anglesey, Gwynedd

Beaumaris, begun in 1295, was the last and the largest of the castles to be built by King Edward I in Wales. Raised on an entirely new site, without earlier buildings to fetter its designer's creative genius, it is possibly the most sophisticated example of medieval military architecture in Britain.

A manuscript illustration of about 1285, showing King Edward I with his senior churchmen (By permission of the British Library, Cotton Ms. Vitellius A XIII, f.6v).

This is undoubtedly the ultimate 'concentric' castle, built with an almost geometric symmetry. Conceived as an integral whole, a high inner ring of defences is surrounded by a lower outer circuit of walls, combining an almost unprecedented level of strength and firepower. Before the age of

The approach to Beaumaris Castle is across a modern wooden bridge leading to the 'Gate next the Sea'.

Beaumaris Castle with the mountains of Snowdonia beyond.

cannon, the attacker would surely have been faced with an impregnable fortress. Yet, ironically, the work of construction was never fully completed, and the castle saw little action apart from the Civil War in the 17th century.

A castle was almost certainly planned when King Edward visited Anglesey in 1283 and designated the Welsh town of Llanfaes to be its seat of government. At the time, resources were already stretched and any such scheme was postponed. Then, in 1294–95, the Welsh rose in revolt under Madog ap Llywelyn. The rebels were crushed after an arduous winter campaign, and the decision was taken to proceed with a new castle in April 1295. The extent of English power is demonstrated by the fact

that the entire native population of Llanfaes was forced to move to a newly established settlement, named Newborough. The castle itself was begun on the 'fair marsh', and was given the Norman-French name *Beau Mareys*. Building progressed at an astonishing speed, with some 2,600 men engaged in the work during the first year.

In sole charge of the operation was Master James of St George, already with many years of experience in castle-building, both in Wales and the Continent. Even after 700 years it is not difficult to appreciate the tremendous sophistication in his elaborate design at Beaumaris. The first line of defence was provided by a water-filled moat, some 18ft wide. At the southern end was a tidal

would have poured down from all directions.

The striking thing about the inner ward is its great size. Covering about ¼ of an acre, it was surrounded by a further six towers and the two great gatehouses. Within, it is clear that there was an intention to provide lavish suites of accommodation. Both gatehouses were planned to have grand arrangements of state rooms at their rear, much as those completed at Harlech. The north gate, on the far side, was only raised as far as its hall level and the projected second storey was never built. Even as it stands, with its five great window openings, it dominates the courtyard. Another block, of equal size, was planned for the south gate, but this was never to rise further than its footings. Around the edges of the ward further buildings were planned and must have included a hall, kitchens, stables and perhaps a granary. Although there is some evidence of their existence in the face of the curtain wall, it is not certain they were ever completed.

Visitors should not miss the little chapel situated in the tower of that name. Its vaulted ceiling and pointed windows make it one of the highlights of the castle. Also in this tower there is a fascinating

dock for shipping, where vessels of 40 tons laden weight could sail right up to the main gate. The dock was protected by the shooting deck on Gunners' Walk.

Across the moat is the low curtain wall of the outer ward, its circuit punctuated by 16 towers and two gates. On the northern side, the Llanfaes gate was probably never completed. The 'Gate next to the Sea', on the other hand, preserves evidence of its stout wooden doors and gruesome 'murder-holes' above. Once through, an attacker would still have to face 11 further obstacles before entering the heart of the castle. These included the barbican, further 'murder-holes', three portcullises and several sets of doors. If the daunting prospect of the gate-passage proved too much,

the would-be attacker caught hesitating between the inner and outer walls could not have survived for long. A rain of heavy crossfire

The almost perfect symmetry and 'concentric' plan of Beaumaris Castle are best seen from the air.

exhibition on the *Castles of Edward I in Wales*, and this provides much background to the building of Beaumaris itself.

The visitor may well be left wondering why all this lavish accommodation was contemplated. In short, it was to provide the necessary apartments for the king and, if he should marry again, his queen. Moreover, his son, the Prince of Wales was fast approaching marriageable age. Considering the size of both households, plus the need to accommodate royal officers, the constable, and even the sheriff of Anglesey, the scale of these domestic arrangements is put into perspective.

Despite being planned on such a grand scale, by 1298 the funds for building Beaumaris had dried up. The king was increasingly involved with works in Gascony and Scotland. Although there were minor building works in later times, the castle is in many ways a blueprint which was never fully realized.

On eastern edge of town. C.   Ae3

MASTER JAMES OF ST GEORGE – THE KING'S CASTLE-BUILDER

As far as Edward I's crucial late 13th-century castle-building programme in Wales was concerned, the architectural power behind the throne was James of St George. James, a little-known but none the less important historical figure, was a master mason summoned from the Continent to implement the king's plans. Born around 1230, he worked on a number of great European castles including the fortress of St Georges d'Espéranche (in Savoy on the French-Swiss-Italian border) from which he took his full name.

Master James was directly responsible for at least 12 of the 17 castles in Wales which Edward either built, rebuilt or helped strengthen. Rhuddlan was James' first venture, Beaumaris his last, by which time he had perfected the symmetrical, concentric 'walls within walls' design which was to characterize the castles of this period.

The king evidently appreciated his work – and knew the worth of such an irreplaceable employee, for he paid James the handsome daily wage of two shillings, an amount which an ordinary craftsman would receive for a whole week's work. In 1284, it rose to three shillings a day for life. In later years, James worked for Edward in Scotland, though he continued to live at a manor in north-east Wales, granted by the king. He died about 1308.

A manuscript illustration of a king and his master mason drawn by Matthew Paris about 1250 (By permission of the British Library, Cotton Nero Ms. D I, f. 23v).

Even after 700 years the moated walls of Beaumaris still present a formidable barrier.

Beaupre Castle – the 'beautiful retreat' of the Basset family in the heart of the Vale of Glamorgan.

BEAUPRE CASTLE, NEAR COWBRIDGE, SOUTH GLAMORGAN

The name Beaupre, derived from the old French *beau-repaire* (beautiful retreat), is a perfect description for this secluded spot in the heart of the pastoral Vale of Glamorgan. The Basset family presumably occupied a medieval house or 'castle' on the site, and there are substantial remains of an early 14th-century hall range on the south of the courtyard, with a former gatehouse and tower of similar date in the south-east corner. Beaupre was, however, largely rebuilt as an Elizabethan mansion in the later 16th century. The outer gate and inner porch represent a fusion of Tudor gothic and early Italian Renaissance styles. The porch, in particular, the work of Sir Richard Basset, is a glorious construction. Richly carved, and carrying Sir Richard's arms on a central shield above the doorway, it is probably the best example of its type in Wales. The courtyard and west range also belong to this late Tudor period.

The adjacent private farmhouse and outbuildings, located to the south, once served as an inner court. It was perhaps the focus of medieval Beaupre, with much surviving from the 14th century.

By footpath, 1m SW of St Hilary, nr Cowbridge. F. **Le6**

The elaborately carved porch built by and displaying the arms of Sir Richard Basset.

BODELWYDDAN CASTLE, BODELWYDDAN, CLWYD

Visitors to this intriguing house, situated near the north Wales coast, are invited to 'join the Victorians for a day out'! Thanks to the initiative of the county council, Bodelwyddan has recently been carefully restored and has become the National Portrait Gallery's regional outstation for Victorian portraits.

Seen from a distance, in its attractive landscape setting, Bodelwyddan has the appearance of a typically sprawling early 19th-century castellated house, peppered with turrets and false arrow-loops. Its origins, however, go back somewhat further, since it is known that there was a house on the site in the 1460s. Between 1800-08, it seems that a somewhat later Elizabethan or early 17th-century building was remodelled in the neo-Classical style for Sir John Williams. Bodelwyddan was further remodelled and enlarged for his son, Sir John Hay Williams, about 1830-42, and it was at this time that the house assumed its castellated appearance.

Apart from the very fine collection of Victorian portraits, there is much of interest inside the house. Parts of the main staircase in the entrance hall are said to be genuine 17th-century work. From here a corridor leads to the great hall, with its elaborate plaster vaulting and a fanciful chimneypiece complete with cast-iron knights in armour. The library also has an unusual chimneypiece, with trees and animals carved in low relief.

The grounds have further attractions, and the gardens are particularly lovely.

2½m W of St Asaph, on A55 (T) C. **Bd4**

The dignified red-bricked manor house of Bodrhyddan Hall.

BODRHYDDAN HALL, NEAR RHUDDLAN, CLWYD

Sir John Conwy, ancestor of the present owner, Lord Langford, completed the oldest part of the present hall in 1696, although a sundial and holy well, found in the extensive grounds, suggest an earlier construction. St Mary's Well, dated 1612, has an octagonal well-house of dressed stone crested with a 'pelican in her piety'.

This dignified, red-bricked manor house contains a fine collection of paintings, furniture and armour, two suits of which are believed to be relics of the Wars of the Roses.

On A5151, 1m E of Dyserth. C.   Be4

BRECON CASTLE, POWYS

On a hill above Brecon's rooftops and the confluence of the Usk and Honddu rivers stands a straggling, impressive ruin, once the centre of power of the medieval lordship of Brycheiniog. A modern road now cuts the site in two. To the south,

the Great Hall put up by Humphrey de Bohun in 1280 is

Brecon Castle.

quite harmoniously integrated with the period architecture of Brecon's Castle Hotel, within the grounds of which the medieval block stands. Across the road, the remains of the 12th-century Ely Tower crown a motte in the garden of the bishop of Swansea and Brecon.

On hill above the town. F.   Ge6

BRECON CATHEDRAL, POWYS

The Normans seized the upper valley of the Usk in the late 11th century, and their leader, Bernard de Neufmarché, established his chief castle at Brecon. About 1110, he was persuaded to create a Benedictine priory as a cell of the vast Sussex abbey at Battle. At the Dissolution of the Monasteries, Brecon survived destruction and continued to serve as a parish church. In 1923 it was chosen as the cathedral of the new diocese of Swansea and Brecon.

Little survives from the earliest Romanesque church, apart from the intriguing font. The east end of the pleasing pinkish-grey building — the chancel — was built under the patronage of William de Braose about 1200-07. The transepts and crossing also date from the 13th century, with the vault completed by Sir Gilbert Scott during the restoration of 1872. The nave was rebuilt with its octagonal piers during the 14th century.

Brecon Cathedral, originally founded as a Benedictine Priory in about 1110.

There are many interesting features and tombs in the cathedral. The Havard Chapel serves as the Regimental Chapel of the South Wales Borderers. In the nave, notice the cresset stone, an unusually large medieval lamp, with holes for 30 oil lights.

Near centre of Brecon. F.   Ge6

BRECON GAER ROMAN FORT, POWYS

The isolated auxiliary fort at Brecon Gaer was vital to the Roman grip on south Wales.

The southern Welsh borderlands probably came under the control of the Roman legions by about AD 55-60. A fortress was established at Usk, and there is evidence for outlying forts at Cardiff and Abergavenny. Further advance was effectively blocked for some years by the fierce resistance put up by the *Silures*, the late Iron Age tribe occupying south-east Wales. They had already defeated a legion in AD 52, and continued to harass all attempts at inroads into

their territory by Roman troops. Although advance parties may have found their way up the arterial valley of the Usk over the next decade or so, Brecon Gaer does not seem to have been established until a series of concerted campaigns between AD 74-78. With a new fortress at Caerleon, the governor Julius Frontinus finally conquered the *Silures* and surrounded their territory with a tight network of forts. Brecon Gaer formed part of this iron grip and was strategically placed at a major junction of east-west and north-south Roman roads. The fort, and later settlement, was known by the Roman name *Cicucium*, and was garrisoned about AD 100 by the Vettonian Spanish cavalry regiment.

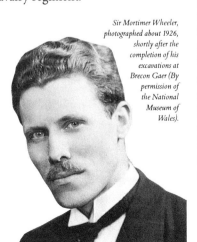

Sir Mortimer Wheeler, photographed about 1926, shortly after the completion of his excavations at Brecon Gaer (By permission of the National Museum of Wales).

The site was first excavated by Sir Mortimer Wheeler in 1924-25, at which time the general outline was recovered. It was quite a large fort for an auxiliary unit, occupying up to 8 acres. The initial defences of the mid 70s comprised an earthen bank with two external ditches. These were replaced about AD 140 by stone walls and gates. The principal buildings within the fort, including the headquarters block, were also rebuilt in stone at this time. In the 3rd century, a bath-house was placed within the defences, perhaps when the size of the garrison had been reduced.

The west and south gates are the best preserved, standing up to 8 ft high. The west gate has projecting towers which are unusual for the period. Parts of the fort wall also survive and include angle turrets at the corners. Wheeler also found evidence for a civilian settlement running north from the north gate. Here the buildings were entirely of timber with clay floors. The fort may have been occupied periodically right through to the end of the 3rd century.

2½m W of Brecon on minor road. In field adjacent to Y Gaer Farm. F.   Gd6

BRONLLYS CASTLE, POWYS

This is one of a dozen or so castles in the southern March, distinguished by its 13th-century round keep. First established as a motte and bailey castle by Richard fitz Pons at the end of the 11th century, the great tower was added by Walter de Clifford III. Such towers were a simple and effective way of bringing a timber castle up to date at this time. The residential rooms with fireplaces may be seen inside. From a now vanished wooden gallery running around the top of the tower, archers could release their lethal fire in all directions. The castle bailey lies under the adjacent house and gardens.

9m NE of Brecon on A479. F.   Ha6

BRYN BRÂS CASTLE, LLANRUG, GWYNEDD

The walls of Bryn Brâs have never been breached by cannon, nor have prisoners languished in dungeons there. This is, in fact, a lavish stately home built as a 'sham' castle about 1830 around an earlier structure, and stands in superb gardens of over 30 acres with walks, pools and waterfalls. Its Romanesque extravagance, however, gives it historic importance as a 19th-century architectural fantasy. Favourite tourist attractions are the drawing room, Louis XV suite, splendid ceilings and galleried staircase. In 1925 Caernarfon iron-workers made ornamental lamps and the coat of arms on the castle archway.

½m off Caernarfon-Llanberis A4086 road at Llanrug. C.   Ad4

The impressive prehistoric burial mound of Bryn Celli Ddu.

BRYN CELLI DDU BURIAL CHAMBER, NEAR LLANFAIR P.G., ISLE OF ANGLESEY, GWYNEDD

A relatively late Neolithic tomb, probably built after 3,000 BC, this is one of the most evocative prehistoric sites in Britain. The mound is partially restored, and was originally up to 85 ft in diameter. A stone lintelled doorway leads into a long covered passage through to the central chamber. A single pillar stone inside was presumably of ritual significance as it serves no structural purpose. One of the wallstones has an incised spiral on its face.

Excavations in the 1920s revealed a long and complex history, and recent research has suggested that the whole mound superseded an earlier henge monument. This ring of stones, surrounded by a bank and ditch, would have been in the same tradition as the much larger Stonehenge. The excavations also recovered cremated and uncremated bones from the burial chamber of the later tomb, and a stone bearing incised meandering decoration was found near the

A replica of the carefully inscribed 'Pattern Stone' at Bryn Celli Ddu. The original is now at the National Museum of Wales.

centre of the mound. A copy of this rare survival can now be seen at the site (the original is at the National Museum of Wales).

Further indications of elaborate ritual were found in front of the entrance, including a pit containing an ox skeleton. Perhaps the monument should be seen not only as a tomb, but also as a temple at which relatives of the dead came to worship and leave gifts.

1m E of Llanddaniel-Fab Church, 2m SW of Llanfair P.G.. F.   Ad3

CAER GYBI ROMAN FORTLET, HOLYHEAD, ISLE OF ANGLESEY, GWYNEDD

The church of St Cybi, in the centre of Holyhead, is surrounded by the walls of a rectangular late-Roman fortlet. Caer Gybi ('Cybi's fort') was probably built in the late 3rd or early 4th century as a base for a small Roman naval flotilla, protecting the Anglesey coast from Irish raiders. As part of the coastal fortification of Wales at this time, it may have been linked to a signal station recently discovered on Holyhead Mountain.

The walls originally had circular towers at all four corners, but that at the south-east was entirely rebuilt in the 19th century. The diagonally laid courses of 'herringbone' masonry in the walls are typical of the late Roman period. There was probably a Roman quay to the east. By the south wall of the fortlet is a small chapel, Eglwys y Bedd ('Church of the Grave'), which is believed to cover the original grave of St Cybi, the 6th-century saint who settled within the deserted fort walls. An Anglo-Saxon silver penny dug up within the churchyard suggests a later use by Viking raiders.

Near harbour in N part of town. F.   Aa2

The well-preserved walls of the Roman fortlet of Caer Gybi.

CAERLEON ROMAN FORTRESS, GWENT

The magnificent remains at Caerleon lay just claim to being one of the largest and most important surviving Roman military sites in Europe. The Romans named their fortress on this site *Isca*, taken from the river hard by, now the Usk. The Welsh used the name 'City of the Legion', and in later translation Caerleon. The 12th-century scholar, Geoffrey of Monmouth, in his *History of the Kings of Britain*, located the crowning of King Arthur at this place, and in legend the remains of the great Roman amphitheatre were 'King Arthur's Round Table'.

Stone dolphin head from the Fortress Baths at Caerleon Roman Fortress.

50 acres. With characteristic Roman efficiency, such legionary strongholds were laid out to a remarkably uniform plan; and *Isca* was no exception. It was originally surrounded by defences of earth and timber, fronted by a wide ditch, but about AD 100 these were replaced by a substantial stone wall. The majority of buildings within

The original layout of the Roman fortress can be seen preserved in the modern street plan of Caerleon.

Today, the streets of the small town overlie those of the mighty fortress. It was established about AD 75 and was the headquarters of the Second Augustan Legion, one of the three legions permanently quartered in the Roman province of *Britannia*. At its peak, the garrison included up to 6,000 men and the fortress covered an area of some

the fortress were also constructed first in wood, but from the 2nd century were gradually rebuilt in stone. They included, in addition to the barracks, a host of other structures ranging from storerooms, to a hospital block, and the extensive Fortress Baths. The legionary headquarters building lies beneath the present parish church.

From this central point, the visitor follows one of the major streets of the fortress towards the south-west gate. To the right, in the area known as Prysg Field, are the only visible remains of Roman legionary barracks in Europe. The fortress originally contained some 64 blocks, and four of these can now be seen. Built in timber soon after the foundation of the fortress, they were rebuilt in stone during the 2nd century. The centurion occupied the slightly broader rooms to one end of each building, with his men in the 12 double cubicles at the narrower part. Eight men were allocated to each pair of cubicles. The larger room provided sleeping accommodation and the smaller served as a kit store. Also visible in this area are examples of early cooking ovens, later cookhouses, and there is a latrine in the far corner.

Just outside the former defences, the oval amphitheatre is one of the best surviving features of the fortress. Built about AD 90, as designed it could seat about 5,000 spectators, and played host to a variety of events and special festivals. Initially, it was intended to build the amphitheatre throughout in stone, though the setting and superstructure were first built in timber; lack of funds meant they never progressed beyond this stage. Nevertheless, from the outset, it seems certain that it was the scene

The celebrated Roman amphitheatre at Caerleon, once believed to be 'King Arthur's Round Table'.

of the grim blood sports so common to Imperial Rome. Gladiatorial combats and animal baiting with bears and wolves could well have taken place in the arena. The amphitheatre was also used for a degree of basic troop training and weapon-practice.

Discovered as recently as 1964, the superb Fortress Baths complex now forms the centrepiece of a visit to Roman Caerleon. A spacious cover-building protects the long, open-air swimming pool (*natatio*), a heated changing room, and part of the cold hall (*frigidarium*) of the baths. The baths were an essential amenity of Roman life, and here they served as a leisure and social centre for the soldiers. They were built soon after AD 75, by an unusually innovative architect, and were to be the showpiece of the new fortress. In sheer mass, with their exercise hall, the baths would have equalled a large medieval cathedral, and seem to have anticipated the design of the vast

Imperial Baths of Rome itself. Much altered and repaired during their history, the buildings went out of use about AD 230. A permanent exhibition at the site uses artists' reconstructions to explain and illuminate the remains.

Sites mentioned are all within the small town of Caerleon, near Newport. C. Mc4

Part of the cold hall which would have held a central cold bath and a pair of flanking basins for a cold splash bath.

Some of the Roman gemstones found during excavations in the drain of the Fortress Baths at Caerleon (By permission of the National Museum of Wales).

CAERNARFON CASTLE, GWYNEDD

When the antiquarian traveller John Taylor visited Caernarfon in the middle of the 17th century, he commented 'if it be well manned, victualled, and ammunitioned, it is invincible'. Indeed, many would argue that it is the greatest of Edward I's castles, and few can doubt that its outward appearance is different from that of any of the other strongholds he commissioned in Wales. Here, King Edward seems to have gone to considerable lengths to give substance to the tradition linking Caernarfon with imperial Rome. The king must have known that the Roman fort of *Segontium*, lying just above the modern town, was inseparably associated in legend with Magnus Maximus, the usurper emperor. Maximus appears as the Macsen Wledig of the *Mabinogion*, and it is *Segontium* which provides the background to his dream of journeying from Rome into a land of high mountains facing an island. There he saw a great city with towers of many colours and eagles fashioned out of gold.

Thus it was that at Caernarfon, the walls were given a prominent patterning with bands of different coloured stone. Moreover, the towers were constructed in an angular fashion rather than the more usual rounded form of, for example, Conwy or Beaumaris. It is difficult to escape the conclusion that Edward I was drawing upon symbolism, and turned for inspiration to the great city of Constantinople. There, in the eastern successor to Rome and one of the wonders of the ancient world, the 5th-century walls bear a striking resemblance to this late 13th-century castle. Overall, the king was creating a fitting building to be a new royal residence, a

An aerial view of King Edward I's magnificent fortress at Caernarfon.

palace, intended to be the seat of government for the newly-formed shire counties of north Wales. Everywhere, strength and majesty are evident in its walls and turrets.

Construction began in June 1283, soon after the final defeat of Llywelyn the Last. As at Conwy, the plan made provision for but a single curtain wall, albeit a massively powerful one. To compensate for this lack of outer defences, the wall was honeycombed by continuous wall-passages at two separate levels. These are all well equipped with arrow-loops and, on the town side, there are lethal multiple embrasures which enabled archers to spread their firepower to terrible effect.

The circuit was punctuated by nine towers and two great gatehouses, though neither of the two gates was ever fully completed. Nevertheless, the visitor who looks carefully at the King's Gate will be left in no doubt as to why it has been described as the mightiest in the land. An attacker would have needed to penetrate no fewer than five hefty doors and six portcullises before entering the heart of the castle. The Queen's Gate lay outside the circumference of the town walls, and would have been approached by way of a high stone ramp and drawbridge. Inside, the plan of Caernarfon is unusual, being shaped rather like an hour

Caernarfon Castle from across the River Seiont.

glass, originally divided into two wards by a cross wall at the narrowest point. In the lower ward are the remains of the great hall and kitchens, but it is the provision of private accommodation in the towers which demands greatest attention.

Most impressive of all is the Eagle Tower, crowned by its triple cluster of turrets. In the 13th century this was almost certainly the residential quarters of Sir Otto de Grandison, King Edward's first Justiciar of North Wales. Everything about it is on a regal scale, each of the turrets

The upper and lower wards of Caernarfon Castle viewed from the top of the Eagle Tower.

The arms of Otto de Grandison.

bearing a stone eagle as further symbolic evidence of the links with imperial power. In addition to the

setting for the Investiture of the present Prince of Wales in July 1969. Since then Prince Charles with his bride, Diana Princess of Wales, have visited Caernarfon on their first joint tour in 1981.

Few castles have such a rich heritage as Caernarfon, and today a visit is made yet more interesting by a number of informative exhibitions and displays throughout the towers. The Eagle Tower houses both an exhibition and audio-visual presentation. All three floors in the Queen's Tower are occupied by the Regimental Museum of the Royal Welch Fusiliers, and there are further exhibitions on the Castles of Edward I and the Princes of Wales in the Chamberlain and North-East Towers.

Nor should the visitor to Caernarfon overlook the remains of the town walls. Built at the same time as the castle, they protected the English inhabitants of the infant borough established by King Edward.

On western end of town overlooking Menai Strait. C.   *Ad4*

accommodation here, Queen's Tower is almost as spacious, and there must have been many more private suites in the Chamberlain, North-East, Granary, and Well Towers.

As the centre for a new seat of government, Caernarfon was clearly marked out for a special role. This was undoubtedly enhanced by the birth, within its precincts, of the first English Prince of Wales. The king's son, Edward of Caernarfon, was born in 1284 and henceforward the castle must have been seen as the palace of a new dynasty of princes. With this in mind, the majestic architecture, together with the extent and quality of accommodation, falls into perspective. Ironically, the castle seldom if ever fulfilled the elevated

role planned for it. As an adult, Prince Edward (later Edward II) never returned to its walls, and by the mid 14th century it had become little more than a depot for the armament of the other north Wales castles.

Even so, it continued to be maintained and garrisoned, and successfully withstood sieges by the forces of Glyndŵr in 1403 and 1404. During the Civil War, Caernarfon finally surrendered to Parliamentary forces in 1646.

Centuries of neglect were halted by repairs undertaken in the late 19th century and, in 1911, it was the scene of the Investiture of Prince Edward (later Edward VIII) as Prince of Wales. Ever since, the castle has been a venue for many royal tours, and was again the

The Royal Welch Fusiliers Museum in the Queen's Tower at Caernarfon.

CAERPHILLY CASTLE, MID GLAMORGAN

The interest and extraordinary impact of Caerphilly derive from its enormous size, together with the complexity of its land and water defences. In all, it covers some 30 acres, and represents the might of medieval military architecture on a majestic scale. Seen mirrored in the still waters of its great lake, or rising mysteriously through a morning mist, the castle presents a prospect rarely surpassed in these islands.

Not surprisingly, the strategic qualities of the site were first recognized by the Romans. During their military conquest of south-east Wales, a fort for about 500 auxiliary soldiers was established at Caerphilly around AD 75. Abandoned some 50 years later, the location was not reoccupied during the early Norman invasion of Glamorgan in the late 11th century. At this time, the new conquerors were content to concentrate on the fertile coastal plains, and the mountainous uplands were left largely to the Welsh. Thus, Caerphilly Mountain effectively

Caerphilly Castle mirrored in its own mighty water defences.

A carefully scaled model of Caerphilly Castle is one of the many displays in an exhibition detailing the history of this impressive fortress.

formed a geographical barrier between Welsh and Anglo-Norman for almost 200 years. Then, in the 1260s, the minor native lords of upland Glamorgan found themselves caught up in the embroilments of national politics. To the north, the ambitious last Welsh prince of Wales, Llywelyn ap Gruffudd, was in effective control of Breconshire and was poised to move further south. But the powerful Marcher lord, Gilbert de Clare, was determined to avoid such a catastrophe, and in 1267 he responded by moving rapidly north. He captured the native ruler, Gruffudd ap Rhys, and in the following year took the opportunity to begin the construction of Caerphilly itself. Although de Clare must have planned a mighty new fortress, it is doubtful that he had

The coat of arms of Gilbert de Clare, the founder of Caerphilly Castle.

any conception of how large and elaborate the finished work would be. Nor was his conflict with Llywelyn over yet. Construction of the formidable defences had scarcely begun before the castle was attacked and burnt by the prince's forces in 1270. Only through skilful negotiation, and the intervention of King Henry III, was full-scale war avoided. On the withdrawal of Llywelyn, de Clare regained Caerphilly and continued building in 1271. It is unlikely that the work was finished at his death in 1295, and operations must have gone on under his son, another Gilbert, who died at the Battle of Bannockburn in 1314.

Caerphilly was built to a 'concentric' design with successive lines of defence set one inside the other, so that when the attacker stormed one line he would find himself face to face with a second. This system of defence saw its fullest development in Edward I's great castles of north Wales. Although the moat is obviously wide and wet enough, and the walls intimidating enough, the defensive principles at the site can only be understood, in their totality, from the air. A seemingly impregnable

series of concentric stone and water defences radiates, in a succession of larger and larger circles, from the central inner ward.

The first line of defence against any attack was the outer moat, spanned by two drawbridges, and backed by a huge curtain wall and gatehouse. The lakes made it almost impossible to use many of the normal methods of siege warfare. Stone-firing catapults could not be brought within range; siege ladders were virtually useless, and it was totally impracticable to tunnel under the waters to undermine the walls.

The inner moat and the gatehouses of the outer ward were the second line of defence. Finally, there stands the very heart of the castle, the inner ward. This is a very large quadrangle enclosed by four curtain walls, with massive round towers at each corner and yet more gatehouses on the east and west sides. These huge gatehouses protect the points of entry and could be shut off and held separately should the rest of the castle fall. That on the east is by far the more impressive, and contained the constable's hall and other accommodation. In design, it set a pattern later adopted by Edward I at Harlech and Beaumaris.

Caerphilly's formidable defences are best viewed from the air where the size and scale of the lakes and central island can be fully appreciated.

A bronze tankard from Caerphilly Castle which may once have graced the table in the Great Hall (By permission of the National Museum of Wales).

From the de Clares, Caerphilly passed to the Despensers, and in 1316 it was attacked during the revolt of Llywelyn Bren. Hugh le Despenser the younger earned the hatred of the Welsh by putting Llywelyn to death in 1318. Unpopular with all save Edward II, Despenser was none the less responsible for the rebuilding of the Great Hall within the inner ward. The work was magnificent, the roof resting on finely carved capitals with portrait busts, and the tall windows decorated with 'ball-flower' ornament. Since its restoration, the hall is one of the highlights of a visit to Caerphilly.

The ill-fated Edward II fled to the castle in 1326, seeking refuge from Queen Isabella and her party. He went on to Margam and Neath, and was eventually captured and imprisoned. His favourite, Despenser, had already been executed. After this time the castle lost its military value and before the

middle of the 16th century it had already fallen into decay. Caerphilly probably saw some further action during the Civil War, but the details are not clear. The effects of gunpowder are perhaps evident in the famous 'leaning tower' of the inner ward. Though equally this could be due to ground subsidence. Whatever the case, this south Wales answer to Pisa adds an unexpected touch to the interest here.

Today, an exhibition in the outer gatehouse tells the story of the castle and surrounding area in some detail. Models, illustrations and an audio-visual programme add to the attractions. Caerphilly also houses an imaginative new *Castles of Wales* exhibition, and the site can now be further enjoyed from a leisurely boat trip on the great lake.

CAERWENT ROMAN TOWN, GWENT

Today, Caerwent is no more than a rural Gwent village, but to the Romans it was *Venta Silurum*, 'the market town of the *Silures*', a warlike tribe whose conquest cost the legions many years of hard fighting. It was established about AD 75-80, soon after the Second Augustan Legion had settled at nearby Caerleon, and became the administrative capital of the former tribal area. An early 3rd-century pedestal, now in the porch of the parish church, carries an inscription recording the setting up of a statue '*by decree of the council, the community of the state of the Silures*'. This rare

A print of a mosaic found in Caerwent in 1855. Many of the houses in the Roman town were decorated with mosaic floors.

The inscription from Caerwent referring to the 'council, the community of the state of the Silures'. The inscription confirms Caerwent's status as a provincial capital.

survival confirms that the now Romanized tribe was a self-governing body.

Initially, the buildings were constructed of wood, but were gradually replaced in stone, and the town grew to cover some 45 acres. The streets were laid out in a regular grid pattern, with houses, shops and public buildings located along the frontages. The *basilica*, or

town hall, lies at the centre of the modern village, just north of the main road. The public baths lay just to the south of this. The massive town walls, still standing up to 17 ft in places, were constructed in the earlier 4th century and bastions were added soon afterwards. In Pound Lane the foundations of two houses are displayed, the southern of which appears to have been owned by a blacksmith for most of its history. Recent excavations have uncovered a large courtyard house, with its mosaics, in the north-west corner of the town, and new evidence has been recovered at the temple and *basilica* sites near the centre of the village.

Although Romanized life was in decline in the surrounding countryside by the later 4th century, Caerwent was occupied well into the 5th century. Some of the later inhabitants were Christians, and there was perhaps some direct continuity through to a 'Dark Age' settlement.

10m SW of Chepstow just off the M4. F.   *Me4*

CALDEY ISLAND MONASTERY, NEAR TENBY, DYFED

In the early days of Christianity in Britain there was a great deal of missionary effort along the western shores, so there was already a long religious tradition on islands like Caldey when monks arrived from the Continent after the Norman Conquest. The Benedictines established a monastery here in the 12th century, and remained until the Dissolution of the Monasteries by Henry VIII. They left solid evidence of their occupation in the buildings that survive from those times — refectory, gatehouse and beautiful little 13th-century church on the site of the island's original monastic settlement. The ancient church contains a monument with an inscription in both Latin and Ogham, a form of ancient lettering which dates from the centuries immediately following the end of Roman occupation.

The Benedictines returned to Caldey and built the present abbey, but in 1929 the Cistercians took over. The Cistercian monks here

The monastery on peaceful and picturesque Caldey Island.

live typically austere lives — male visitors to the island are invited to take a guided tour of their simple dwellings. But the monks are not without an astute awareness of the vanities of the secular world: they make scent from the island's flowers and sell it to visitors. A trip to this beautiful island, far removed from the pressures of the workaday world, is an enriching experience.

> *Reached by regular boat service from Tenby harbour in summer. C.* Je6

CALDICOT CASTLE, GWENT

Caldicot stands on a fortified site of great antiquity, two miles from the sea and on the route of the Roman road *Via Julia*, which ran to Caerwent. The lords of the castle can be traced back to Norman times. The keep was probably built by Humphrey de Bohun after he inherited the lordship in 1221. The curtain wall came next, though it was not until the 14th century that Caldicot's finest feature — its Great Gatehouse — was put up. This dates from the time of Thomas Woodcock, son of King Edward III, who married Eleanor de Bohun and proceeded to lavish money on the castle in the 1380s. The Woodcock

Tower, a smaller gatehouse, is quite simple in comparison to the well-appointed Great Gatehouse, the hall of which now serves as a magnificent setting for medieval banquets.

Little-known Caldicot is a castle full of architectural interest, deserving of a wider audience (there is also a fine local museum on site). It was sympathetically restored in the last century by wealthy antiquarian J.R. Cobb.

> *5m SW of Chepstow off the M4 at junction 22. C.* Me4

CAPEL GARMON BURIAL CHAMBER, NEAR LLANRWST, GWYNEDD

This well preserved Neolithic tomb is a far-flung member of the group archaeologists call 'Cotswold-Severn', named after the area where they chiefly occur. Excavated in 1924, Capel Garmon perhaps dates to about 3,500 BC, though it is only possible to speculate on why its form should resemble that of tombs further south. The excavations revealed a wedge-shaped cairn, surrounded by a revetment wall, and with 'horns' extending on either side of a false entrance at the east end. The true entrance is on the south side, from which a passage some 16ft long leads to the triple burial chamber itself. A large capstone survives above the west compartment. When complete, these details could not have been seen as the whole was intentionally buried beneath the barrow mound.

> *5m S of Llanrwst off minor road. F.* Bb6

Caldicot Castle. Its finest feature is the Great Gatehouse dating from the time of Thomas Woodcock, son of King Edward III.

CARDIFF CASTLE, SOUTH GLAMORGAN

The castle as it stands today owes more to the spirit of romance than to historical accuracy, for it is essentially the creation of a Victorian architect, William Burges, who transformed the dreams of his patron, the third marquess of Bute, into reality. It is,

John Patrick Crichton Stuart, the third marquess of Bute (By permission of the National Museum of Wales).

however, a splendid and memorable period piece, and its position in the heart of the Welsh capital gives the main shopping streets an unusual focus. Not that the castle lacks any history: it is in reality a unique three-in-one historic site, part Roman, part Norman, part Victorian. The flamboyant creation masterminded by Burges and Bute occupies the site of a Roman fort, and a Norman keep survives to sound an authentic medieval note.

Cardiff Castle, where the curtain wall still follows the line of the Roman defences.

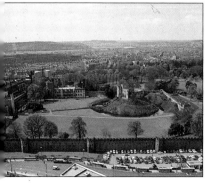

The Norman shell keep still dominates Cardiff Castle today.

The Roman fort was a simple affair with ditch and embankment, set on the tidal estuary of the Taff, and the present castle follows the outline of that eight-acre walled enclosure.

The Normans, cashing in on the strategic value of the site, used what remained of the old Roman defences as a framework for a fortress which had as its strong point — a motte, or mound — crowned with a palisade. Welsh resistance to their foreign masters gave rise to a breathtaking escapade by Ifor Bach, ruler of Senghennydd, who stormed the keep in 1158, carried off the Norman lord and his wife and held them captive until redress had been made for injustices inflicted on the people.

Towards the end of the 13th century the castle was extended by Gilbert de Clare, who rebuilt the gatehouse tower of the keep and constructed the great central wall linking it with the Black Tower.

As old enmities relaxed, spacious living apartments

A thirteenth-century costrel — a medieval 'hip flask' — used for storing cider or beer, from Cardiff Castle (By permission of the National Museum of Wales).

appeared along the west wall of the castle, and piecemeal alteration over the centuries eventually led to the wholesale reconstruction by Burges between 1867 and 1875. The richly ornamented Clock Tower, 150 ft high, belongs to this period, and so do the Guest Tower, and guest rooms and the Octagonal Tower, with its wooden spire. The exterior of the castle is quaint and attractive but it is only when one looks inside that one realizes just how much money and effort went into the satisfaction of the whims of the marquess of Bute. The lavishly decorated rooms represent the spirit of medieval romance, no less; but they also summarize the immense self-confidence of the

The fireplace in the Banqueting Hall at Cardiff, depicting Robert the Consul, duke of Gloucester.

Victorians. The names of some of the rooms have a period quaintness: the Bachelors' Bedroom, the Arab Room, the Chaucer Room. Grandeur and over-statement go hand-in-hand with a certain naivety and artistic delicacy: an engaging combination. The main points of interest in the castle, which was handed over to the city of Cardiff by the Bute family in 1948, are as follows:

Clock Tower: A carved figure of the Devil is above the arch of the door leading into the tower. The stairway leads us to the Winter Smoking Room, where the fireplace was carved on site from a single block of Forest of Dean stone. It bears the Stuart coat of arms, above which is the figure of Diana, the Huntress. On the ceiling the central boss, representing the sun, stands amid the 12 signs of the Zodiac. Above this room is the Bachelors' Bedroom, where the overmantel displays are the Crichton-Stuart coat of arms surmounted by the Crown of Scotland — the Butes are a Scottish family. Fragments of rocks found on the Bute estate are set around the fireplace, and precious stones are inlaid in the wall and stained-glass windows. The marble bath in the adjoining bathroom is of Roman origin and bears intriguing designs of fish.

On the topmost flight of the tower one finds the Summer Smoking Room, where the figure of a chained dragon guards the entrance door. A bronze model of the world, set in tiles, is inlaid in the centre of the floor, and the large chandelier represents the sun. The capitals of the pillars supporting the gallery symbolize the winds. Beautiful hand-painted tiles on the wall illustrate classical themes, such as Hercules slaying the lion and Psyche opening her eyes on Cupid.

The Herbert Tower: This is the most southerly of the projecting towers along the west wall and was probably built in the 16th century, but the Arab Room dates from 1881. It is mock Moorish, with a gilded ceiling and cupboards of cedarwood. A chimney-piece of white marble inset with lapis lazuli is the chief treasure.

The Banqueting Hall: The exploits of Robert the Consul, the natural son of Henry I, are depicted in the murals in this hall, which is the most important room in the castle. Robert succeeded to the lordship of Glamorgan by marriage about 1120 and was closely involved in the power struggle which followed the accession to the throne of Matilda, daughter of Henry I, in 1135. Playing his cards shrewdly, if not always honourably, he fought first on one side and then on the other. The shields on the ceiling of the Banqueting Hall bear the arms of the families who figure in the Bute ancestry.

The Summer Smoking Room in the Clock Tower at Cardiff.

The Arab Room in the Herbert Tower (1876–89) at Cardiff.

The Library: The stained-glass windows have Biblical themes and the doorways are decorated with heraldic emblems of animal figures. Fine craftsmanship has gone into the panelled doors and bookcases.

The Entrance Hall: A royal touch: stained-glass windows showing the castle in the past. Part of the original Roman wall is visible. Cardiff's Roman ancestry is also recalled in a 100-yard long mural of epic proportions, created beneath the old foundations, which depicts life here before and during the Roman occupation. The castle is also the home of the Welch Regiment's Museum, and medieval banquets are held in the cellars.

The Octagonal Tower: The Scottish theme persists here, too. The lion rampant of the arms of Scotland is depicted at the foot of the staircase. There are shields over the doors, and scenes from Aesop's Fables are shown in painted insets on the staircase. At the top of the tower is the Chaucer Room, with its stained-glass windows illustrating the Canterbury Tales. Note the oak panelling with its designs of wild flowers inlaid with mother-of-pearl. The floor has an interesting design in the form of a maze, and the chimney-piece of Milan marble is dominated by the figure of Chaucer.

The Chapel: A room with sad associations. It was the dressing-room of the second marquess of Bute until he died here suddenly in 1848; later it was made into a private chapel, and a bust of the marquess marks the spot where he died. The Tree of Life is carved on one side of the door and a fallen tree, illustrating the frailty of life, on the other.

The Dining Room: The ceiling is richly decorated in gold leaf. Note the curious bell-push: a monkey holding an acorn in its mouth.

In city centre. C.   Mb5

CARDIGAN CASTLE, DYFED

A convoluted, complex history and at least one change of location characterize this tumbledown castle overlooking the River Teifi. Lord Rhys, a Welsh ruler whose domain extended throughout west Wales at the height of his power, apparently fortified the castle in stone. When the Norman baron William Marshall arrived on the scene, he began rebuilding the castle. A new keep and town walls were added in 1250, after which Edward I based a local seat of administration here. The site has been partially built over, so its exact dimensions are hard to assess.

On high buff within the town. Not open to public. View from surrounding area.   Fa5

The magnificent ceiling in the Arab Room in Cardiff's Herbert Tower.

The fine Tudor mullioned windows are a notable feature at Carew Castle.

CAREW CASTLE, DYFED

Admirers of Carew claim it as the most attractive castle in south-west Wales, and while this may be disputed there is no denying its handsome appearance — or the beauty of its setting. It stands above the tidal waters of the River Carew on a low limestone outcrop, with meadows on either side. Carew was built between about 1280 and 1310 to replace a simple motte-and-bailey Norman structure, and one must remember that the mill dam below, which now inhibits access by water, is of more recent origin. The west front is typical of a medieval fortress, with two round towers of immense strength. Their massive spur buttresses, which rise to first floor level, are the most striking architectural features of Carew, and have their nearest parallel at Goodrich in Herefordshire.

The castle is also important for its unique medieval 'maisonettes' used by the constable and chaplain of the garrison. Carew was enlarged considerably in the 15th century, when the great hall was built, and the fortress became a fine and comfortable Tudor residence (its mullioned windows, for example, are a decorative delight). Reconstruction work was carried out by Sir John Perrot, reputedly the natural son of Henry VIII, who also made extensive alterations at Laugharne Castle.

The ample cellars at Carew suggest that the occupants of the castle appreciated the good things of this life. There was at least one fireplace in all the larger rooms, and there also appears to have been more garderobes than one would normally expect to find in a castle of this period. Architecturally it bridges the gulf between the primarily military castles of the late 13th century and the fortified manor houses of the 15th century.

On A4075, 3m E of Pembroke. C. Jd6

CAREW CROSS, DYFED

Standing near the entrance to Carew Castle, this is one of the finest 11th-century crosses in Britain, and represents a milestone in the history of Welsh art. It stands nearly 14 ft high, and is of two parts with a wheel-head at the top fitted into position by a tenon. The swastika and plaitwork patterns on the lower shaft reveal both Celtic and Viking influence, and reveal a sculptor of considerable technical achievement. The inscription bears the name of Margiteut, who is thought to be Maredudd ap Edwin, king of Deheubarth (south-west Wales) from 1033 until his death in battle in 1035. Thus, it is almost certain that the cross was erected soon after this date.

Today, the distinctive wheel-head of the Carew cross provides the inspiration for the symbol of Cadw: Welsh Historic Monuments.

Carew Cross, depicting the cross-cultural links between Viking and Celtic art.

Situated by the gates of Carew Castle. F.   *Jd6*

CARMARTHEN CASTLE, DYFED

A Norman stronghold, probably sited down river from this site, was eventually superseded by this hilltop castle guarding a crossing point on the River Tywi. We know that Edward I restored it at a cost of £169.15s.3d. Additional extensions in the 14th century included the King's Hall and the Queen's Apartment.

The most significant remains are the motte and gateway, flanked by imposing twin towers. Excavations have exposed further stretches of the castle walls, thus improving the general appearance of the site. The castle is thought to stand close to the site of the Romans' most westerly fort in Wales (though the fort has not been identified archaeologically). On the eastern approach to Carmarthen is an excavated Roman amphitheatre.

In town centre. F.   Kc2

CARREG CENNEN CASTLE, NEAR LLANDEILO, DYFED

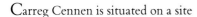

Carreg Cennen is situated on a site of spectacular defensive qualities. Striking and powerful, it commands a great limestone crag nearly 300 ft above the Cennen valley. Although such a location may well have been used as a stronghold from early times, the castle first appears in written sources of the mid 13th century. In 1277 it was prised from Welsh hands by the forces of Edward I, and following the king's eventual conquest of Gwynedd, it was granted to John Giffard. Most of the surviving buildings date from the later 13th to early 14th centuries, and belong to Giffard's time or that of his son. However, following a Welsh revolt, in 1287 it was placed in the care of the earl of Hereford for two years. The construction of the inner ward bears many hallmarks of this period.

Carreg Cennen illustrates many of the principles of fortification refined in the great castles of Edward I in north Wales. In particular, its plan is based on the use of one set of defences inside another. The inner ward is earliest, and is dominated by the powerful gatehouse with arrow-slits at all levels. Notice the single round tower on the north-west corner. Within the ward, the main residential block lies to the left, with the hall on the first floor and a chapel in the upper part of a small projecting tower. The gatehouse was subsequently strengthened with the addition of a barbican, consisting of a long stepped ramp, guarded by gates and pits below moveable bridges. The outer ward was the last to be built, extending down the hilltop and having solid round watch-towers at the corners. A fascinating feature at Carreg Cennen is the narrow vaulted passage which runs some 30 yards along the cliff face from the south-east corner of the inner ward. It leads to a natural cave, used in part as a dovecot. The cave had to be included in the castle's defences to prevent attackers establishing themselves there under cover.

The castle eventually passed to the Duchy of Lancaster, though following the accession of the Yorkist Edward IV, a number of Lancastrian power bases in south Wales were brought to order. In 1462 some 500 men armed with picks and crowbars set about the destruction of Carreg Cennen on behalf of the king.

4½m SE of Llandeilo. Access by 2/300 yard footpath from carpark. C.   La1

Carreg Cennen — perched on a rocky crag, high above the Cennen valley.

CASTELL COCH, NEAR CARDIFF, SOUTH GLAMORGAN

This enchanting castle, a combination of Victorian fantasy and timeless fairytale, is truly astonishing. As if in some alpine setting, its conical turrets peep above the beech woodland on a steep hillside overlooking a gorge in the Taff valley. Castell Coch (the 'red castle') is quite simply one of the most romantic, if unexpected, buildings in Wales.

A Victorian dream translated into stone, it was the creation of the fabulously wealthy third marquess of Bute and his friend, the brilliant but eccentric William (Billy) Burges. These two, patron and architect, had already embarked upon the rebuilding and glorious transformation of Cardiff Castle. Then, in 1871, Lord Bute asked Burges to carry out a survey and make proposals for Castell Coch. The result was a report in which Burges outlined a scheme for a highly imaginative reconstruction of the 13th-century castle on the

William Burges, the creative genius who designed the architecture and decoration of Castell Coch (By courtesy of the Illustrated London News).

The fairytale turrets of Castell Coch peeping out from the surrounding beech woodland.

The splendid vaulted drawing room ceiling where great gold ribs fall amongst birds, butterflies and stars in the sky.

Dining Room and the rooms in the Keep Tower are the most richly decorated, with the passions of saints, Aesop's fables, birds, butterflies, monkeys, other beasts and flowers. Mythology, too, is represented, with the Three Fates above the chimney-piece in the drawing room, and the winged figure of Psyche in Lady Bute's bedroom. This latter room is perhaps the most spectacular, with its domed and mirrored ceiling revealing Burges at his most fanciful.

An original well gives its name to a further tower, and there is a final touch in the steps leading down to a gloomy dungeon. An exhibition in the base of the Kitchen Tower tells more of Castell Coch, of Burges and of Lord Bute.

Just off the A470 at Tongwynlais, approx. 5m NW of Cardiff. C.   Ma5

A decorative detail from Aesop's Fables in the drawing room — The Fox and the Crow.

site. Work began in 1875 and the framework was finished by 1879. Sadly, Burges died suddenly in 1881, and it took a further 10 years to complete the interior decoration and fittings.

The resulting castle is a decorative extravaganza. Though the turrets may appear French,

every detail of military construction was firmly based on medieval precedents, right down to the 'murder-holes' and portcullis at the entrance. Inside, Burges's architecture and decoration are a feast to the eye. Always there is something else to see, at once both surprising and captivating. The

Lady Bute's bedroom where the decorative theme is 'The Sleeping Beauty'.

CASTLES OF THE 19TH CENTURY

Do not be fooled by appearances. Not all castles are what they may seem. Not all castles have seen active service, stood the test of time or survived the ravages of climate through the ages. Some of Wales' most imposing monuments are, in fact, no more than 100-150 years old.

Look again at them. Their towers seem almost too perfect. Their crenellated battlements crown highly decorative, even fanciful, façades, far removed from the purely functional, purely military masonry of an authentic medieval castle.

Fairytale Castell Coch, ornate Cardiff and sturdy Penrhyn are three of the so-called 'sham' castles built during the 19th century from fortunes created by the Industrial Revolution (in Cardiff's case it was coal, in Penrhyn's slate). They reflect the aspirations of the nouveau riche industrialist intent on broadcasting his newly-found wealth — and its hopeful corollary, status — to the world at large. As such, they tell us far more about 19th-century society than 13th-century conflict, though their architecture and decor were in many cases, infused with a vision, albeit highly romantic, of medieval times.

59

Castell Dinas Brân, sited in ancient Iron Ages defences.

CASTELL DINAS BRÂN, LLANGOLLEN, CLWYD

An ancient and almost impregnable stronghold of the Welsh princes probably built just before 1270 by Madog, prince of this part of Powys. The builders made cunning use of the natural defences afforded by the steep drop to the north and west — and also of the leftovers from an original Iron Age hillfort on the site. Modern students of architecture and civil engineering will admire the skill and resourcefulness of its construction. To the east and south, where the slopes are more gentle than on the precipitous north and west sides, a deep ditch was hewn out of the solid rock — and the displaced rock provided most of the stone for the castle. Two long and narrow towers flanked the vaulted passage of the entrance at the north-east angle, and a barbican provided extra protection. The living quarters next to the hall contained a solar or drawing-room where the commander of the castle enjoyed his draughts of mead as he listened to the poetry and song of the wandering bards and harpists.

The more literally-minded have been puzzled by the question of how the castle obtained its water supply. The answer appears to be that the limestone formed such a good, natural reservoir a few feet below the surface that the occupants did not have to look around for springs to supplement the rainfall. In fact, two wells have been found at Dinas Brân. After the English conquest the castle fell so rapidly into decay that it played no part in the Owain Glyndŵr uprising early in the 15th century.

1m NE of town — cross Dee bridge and canal and follow signposted footpath. F.　　　　　　*Ec1*

Castell Henllys Iron Age Fort, near Eglwyswrw, Dyfed

An adventurous and innovative historical exercise is taking place here, on the site of an authentic Iron Age promontory fort. Castell Henllys was inhabited in the Romano-Celtic period, from around 300 BC. Celtic prehistory is brought to life here by archaeologists and a 'reconstruction' team, whose aim it is to reproduce working and living conditions as they were in the Iron Age and afterwards.

A whole range of ancient skills and practices take place here, based around a reconstructed Iron Age hut. Crops are planted and sheep are kept, much as they were 2,000 years ago. Thatching, weaving, dyeing, potting, wattling and daubing are some of the early village crafts on display here, and visitor participation is encouraged. The entire site is still being excavated, with plans for further reconstructions.

A few miles W of Eglwyswrw, nr Cardigan, off A487. C.   *Je2*

A reconstructed Iron Age round house at Castell Henllys.

Castell y Bere on its well-appointed rocky island in the Dysynni valley, once a stronghold of Llywelyn the Great.

Castell y Bere, near Abergynolwyn, Gwynedd

Deep in the mountainous heart of mid Wales, nestling at the foot of Cader Idris, lie the ruins of Castell y Bere. An atmospheric site, it is an outstanding example of a stronghold of the native Welsh princes, and an illuminating contrast with the castles of their English adversaries. Almost certainly begun in 1221 by Llywelyn the Great, who had taken Meirionnydd from his son, Gruffudd, and 'began to build a castle there for himself', it was presumably an attempt by the prince to exert his authority and claims to the southern boundary of Gwynedd.

Situated in the upper Dysynni valley, the shape of the castle is dictated by the isolated rock outcrop on which it stands. The entrance was once quite elaborate, defended by deep rock-cut ditches and drawbridges. At the northern and southern ends of the ridge are two D-shaped towers, characteristic of native Welsh castles. The southern one, standing alone, probably contained private apartments, and could have held out as a last resort if the courtyard had fallen. Finds of highly decorated stonework in the tower to the north suggest that it contained a chapel on the first floor. A rectangular tower on the summit of the ridge seems to have formed a central strongpoint, or keep.

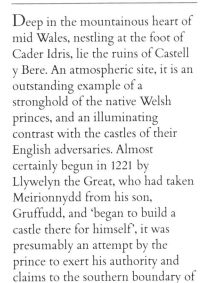

A reconstructed medieval wooden bucket from remains found at Castell y Bere. (By permission of the National Museum of Wales)

Castell y Bere fell to the forces of Edward I in 1283, and was to some extent refortified. Susequently garrisoned for the king, it was abandoned after the Welsh uprising of 1294. Today, the scenes of siege and warfare seem centuries away from the tranquility and beauty of this location.

Few miles N of Abergynolwyn on minor road to Llanfihangel-y-pennant. F.   *Db5*

Chepstow Castle, high above the River Wye, defended one of the main routes from southern England into Wales.

CHEPSTOW CASTLE, GWENT

Superbly set high upon its river cliff above the Wye, Chepstow still guards one of the main river crossings from southern England into Wales. Few castles in Britain tell the story of medieval fortification, from beginning to end, as does this mighty stronghold. It was probably the very first stone castle in the entire country, and was to see successive developments right through to the Civil War of the 17th century. Throughout the Middle Ages, Chepstow was the centre of military and administrative power in the Marcher lordship of *Strigoil*.

Within a few months of the Battle of Hastings, William fitz Osbern, lord of Breteuil in Normandy, was created earl of Hereford by William the Conqueror, and was given the task of subduing the southern Welsh borderlands. Before his death in 1071 he had built the rectangular stone keep, which still forms the core of the castle today. It is the earliest datable secular stone building in Britain, but is very similar to other 11th-century hall-keeps in Normandy or the Loire valley. Notice that the builders used several bands of red Roman tile in the construction, probably robbed from the ruins of Caerwent. The small round-headed windows in the ground floor are also original features.

The opening of the Gloucestershire section of the Domesday Book, recording that 'Earl William built the castle of Chepstow' (Copyright: Public Record Office, from Domesday facsimile, f. 162a, RR 15/96).

William fitz Osbern's hall-keep (the Great Tower), which is the earliest datable stone secular building in Britain.

The interior of the barbican at Chepstow Castle.

At the end of the 12th century, Chepstow passed by marriage to William Marshall, a formidable soldier of fortune, and earl of Pembroke. With considerable experience of military architecture in France, he set about bringing fitz Osbern's castle up to date. He rebuilt the east curtain wall, with two round towers projecting outwards, in order to protect this vulnerable side. Arrow-slits in the towers were designed to give covering fire to the ground in front of the curtain, and this was one of the earliest examples of the new defensive mode which was to become characteristic of the medieval castle.

Before 1245, the sons of William Marshall greatly enlarged Chepstow's defences and improved the internal accommodation. They added a new lower bailey, with an impressive twin-towered gatehouse. At the upper end of the castle, a strongly defended barbican was constructed at this time. Marshall's sons also made additions to the Great Tower, or keep.

Between 1270-1300 Roger Bigod III, one of the greatest magnates of his day, built a splendid new hall block on the north side of the lower bailey. The range includes a large vaulted cellar, elaborate service rooms, a kitchen, domestic accommodation and, of course, the hall itself. There is also a latrine set spectacularly high over the river cliff. Across the bailey, away from the noise of the hall and the kitchen smells, Bigod built a huge new tower on the south-east corner. This was to provide a suite of accommodation worthy of a nobleman of high rank. As well as the domestic apartments, Marten's Tower also included a private chapel, with richly carved decoration and a seat at either side for the priest. Unusually, when raised, the portcullis closing off the wall-walk below would have stood in front of the altar. Roger Bigod was also responsible for the construction of the splendid 'Port', or town wall which still survives

along much of its length.

Chepstow was further modified in the Tudor period, and in the Civil War it was twice besieged. Its defences, designed against medieval attack, fell both times to Parliamentary cannon. Following the war, the whole southern face of the castle was reinforced with earth and stone as a prevention against further cannon fire. The parapets were remodelled with musket loops. Chepstow was also used for State prisoners at this time, and the republican and regicide, Henry Marten, spent 20 years of fairly comfortable captivity in the tower which now bears his name.

Overlooking the River Wye
N of town centre. C.   *Me3*

The exterior of the barbican wall which forms the south-western defences of the castle.

CHIRK CASTLE, CLWYD

Founded by Edward I, this is no romantic ruin but a stately home of great elegance and style. It has been extensively altered over the centuries, and has been in the hands of the Myddelton family since 1595. It is unique amongst Edwardian fortresses in boasting continuous occupancy right up to present times and, as such, displays the hallmarks of many different architectural styles and generations.

A border castle, Chirk stands on a hill and commands fine views across Cheshire to the Pennines. The entrance gates are a particularly fine example of 18th-century craftsmanship, with their elaborate tracery. The cage posts enclose beautiful flowering plant designs, and the intricate crestings are another triumph. The gates, which were the work of Robert and Thomas Davies of Bersham, near Wrexham, were made between 1719 and 1721 and originally stood on the north side of the castle.

The gates to Chirk Castle – a magnificent display of eighteenth-century craftsmanship.

The richly furnished salon in Chirk Castle – particularly notable for its ornately carved and gilded panel mouldings.

In style, the castle, with its circular corner towers, was akin to that of other Edwardian castles in Wales. It was completed in 1310. The neo-Gothic Cromwell Hall, with oak-panelled walls and panelled ceiling, is the work of Pugin, who carried out extensive alterations in the east range in the 1840s. Arms and armour from the times of the Civil War are on display, constituting one of the few surviving 17th-century armouries. Beyond this room, all the elegance of the 18th century is captured in the staircase fashioned in the style of Robert Adam. A portrait of Sir Thomas Myddelton, a merchant adventurer and partner in the buccaneering expeditions of Sir Walter Raleigh to the Spanish Main, and who bought the castle in 1595, stands at the foot of the stairs.

The state dining room, restored to its original 18th-century colours in 1963, has a brass and crystal chandelier and carved marble chimneypiece which typify the period. In the richly furnished salon, note the carved and gilded panel mouldings and the pair of Dresden candelabra on the centre table. Throughout the castle, there are a wealth of fine paintings, as well as many other superb rooms, including a Tudor Block containing a part of the building unchanged since Elizabethan times. A deep dungeon and 18th-century servants' hall are among the more out-of-the-way attractions here. Chirk, in the ownership and care of The National Trust, stands in magnificent 468-acre parklands.

1m W of Chirk. C.   Ec1

Cilgerran Castle, Dyfed

Cilgerran stands perched on a rocky crag, overlooking a steep gorge of the River Teifi. It is a site which cannot fail to stir the imagination, and the location was much favoured by artists of the 18th and 19th centuries. Over 200 years ago tourists were visiting the ruins on boat trips along the river from Cardigan, and it has remained an attraction ever since. Traditionally, the castle is associated with romance, for in the early 12th century it was the home of Nest, Gerald of Windsor's wife — 'the Helen of Wales'. Owain, the son of the prince of Powys, fell in love with her, and such was his ardour that in 1109 he attacked and burnt the castle and abducted her, setting all Wales aflame. At the time, Cilgerran was probably built

Cilgerran Castle, built largely by William Marshall the younger after he finally wrested the site from Welsh hands.

of earth and timber. In 1164 it was taken from the Normans by the Lord Rhys of Deheubarth. Recaptured in 1204 by William Marshall, earl of Pembroke, it fell once more under assaults led by Llywelyn the Great.

William Marshall the younger finally wrested Cilgerran from Welsh hands in 1223, and began construction of the powerful stone castle which survives today. Two massive round towers, with stretches of curtain wall, stand behind a rock-cut ditch. The towers had four storeys, and the walls facing the attacking side are some 4 ft thicker than the rest. On the second floor of each, a door led on to the battlemented wall-walk. Between the towers, a small doorway through the curtain was protected by a portcullis operated from the battlements. The main gatehouse lies next to the west tower. It had a portcullis at either end of the passage, and there may have been a chapel above.

Later in the 13th century, a square tower and thick curtain walls were added to the other side of the inner ward. By 1275 the castle was apparently derelict, but was refortified on the orders of Edward III in 1377. It remained in use, and following the Wars of the Roses was occupied by the Vaughan family, perhaps until the end of the 16th century.

Cilgerran Castle perched on a rocky cliff overlooking the River Teifi.

3m S of Cardigan. C.

Fa6

Coity — one of the finest castles in the Southern March.

northern extension to the keep.
Coity was gradually abandoned in
the late 16th century.

*Off the A4061 2m NE of
Bridgend. C.*   Ld5

COLD KNAP ROMAN BUILDING, BARRY, SOUTH GLAMORGAN

In the summer of 1980, on the foreshore at Cold Knap, Barry, a remarkable story gradually unfolded. The site had been chosen for new housing, but earlier indications of a Roman building here had led archaeologists to keep a close eye on such developments. Encouraged by traces of wall tops, work began on uncovering what emerged as a large building of 21 rooms arranged around an open courtyard. So important was the discovery, the building was saved from the clutches of development, and was consolidated and laid out for public display.

The exact function of this intriguing Roman site has not been fully resolved. It was, however, probably constructed in the late 3rd or early 4th century during the reign of the self-proclaimed emperor Carausius. Its position on the coast, with excellent views across the Bristol Channel, begs the question of maritime association. One explanation is that it formed part of a *mansio*, the equivalent of a modern inn, where officials could await a ship on the correct tide. Alternatively, it may have been linked to a series of defences and installations, strengthened or introduced around the south Wales shore at this time.

*Near the Knap, just W of
Barry Island. F.*   Ma6

COITY CASTLE, BRIDGEND, MID GLAMORGAN

Coity was the centre of an important Norman lordship, held by the Turbervilles under the greater lord of Glamorgan. The initial stronghold was almost certainly thrown up by Payn de Turberville, who in tradition married the heiress of the earlier Welsh lords and thereby secured the lands without bloodshed. Payn's castle was an earthen 'ringwork', with a timber palisade crowning the bank, and surrounded by a circular ditch. Towards the end of the 12th century, it was probably Gilbert de Turberville who converted the defences to stone, building a powerful square keep and a curtain wall following the line of the earlier bank. Coity was, however, largely remodelled in the 14th century, some of which was the work of Sir Lawrence Berkerolles who had inherited the estates. It was at this time that the outer ward received a stone wall,

with square towers at the angles. A new tower was added to the south of the keep, and the middle gate fashioned between the two. Inside the inner ward, a new range of buildings was constructed against the curtain which included a hall and chapel, both on the first floor. The east gate, defended by drawbridge and portcullis, was also added at this time and led out to the church.

Sir Lawrence withstood a long siege during the Welsh uprising under Owain Glyndŵr. Further alterations were made in the Tudor period, including the addition of a third storey to the hall block, and a

An Islamic form of pharmaceutical mortar, found at Coity, which may have been brought back from a Crusade. (By permission of the National Museum of Wales)

Conwy is by any standards one of the great fortresses of medieval Europe. First impressions are of tremendous military strength, a dominating position and a unity and compactness of design. The eight mighty towers seem to spring from the very rock which dictated the castle's eventual layout. As with Edward I's other great castles in north Wales, the design and building operations were in the hands of James of St George, who eventually held the title of Master of the King's Works in Wales. At Conwy, however, he somehow created a building which, more than any other, demonstrates his brilliant understanding of military architecture.

It was during his second campaign in Wales that King Edward gained control of the Conwy valley in March 1283. He began work on the new fortress almost immediately, the natural advantages of the site being far superior to those of the older castle at Deganwy on the opposite side of the estuary. Moreover, plans were laid for an accompanying garrison town, itself to be defended by a complete circuit of walls and towers. Castle and town walls were all built in a frenzied period of activiy between 1283-87, a tremendous achievement in which up to 1,500 craftsmen and labourers were involved during peak periods.

Unlike most of the king's other new castles in Wales, Conwy was not built to a 'concentric' plan. The nature of the rock outcrop dictated a linear outline, with a lower barbican outwork at each end. The interior was sharply divided by a cross wall into two quite separate wards, so that either could hold out independently if the other should fall. When completed, the walls would have been covered with a white plaster rendering, which must have had a stunning effect, quite different from the grey stonework visible today. Traces of this can be seen clinging to the outer walls.

The original entrance to the outer ward was by way of a long stepped ramp up to the west barbican, which was defended by drawbridge and portcullis. Inside the ward, the four towers provided some accommodation for the garrison, and in the base of the Prison Tower is the gloomy dungeon. On the left the foundations mark the site of the kitchens and stables. To the right, the unusual bowed plan of the Great Hall was made necessary by the rocky foundation. Some 125 ft long, it dominates the outer ward, and with its fine windows and original bright decoration it must have appeared a glorious sight during royal feasts.

At the far end of the ward is the castle wall, and beyond this a further drawbridge protected the entrance to the inner ward. This was the heart of the castle, the area occupied by the private apartments of the king and queen. They included a hall and sumptuous presence chamber, though only the shells of the once magnificent windows remain to give some indication of their former splendour. Notice that the towers

Conwy from the air, dominated by the castle and surrounded by the impressive town walls.

are crowned by turrets where the royal standards would have been raised when Edward and Queen Eleanor were in residence. A beautiful little chapel gives one tower its name, and the King's Tower provided further private rooms.

The east barbican was approached from the river, by way of a water gate. This gave added security to the royal apartments, whereas the barbican itself was occupied by a small garden planted at the request of the queen.

King Edward was actually beseiged at Conwy during the rebellion of Madog ap Llywelyn in 1295. Though food ran low, the walls stood firm. Some alterations were carried out under Edward, the Black Prince, in the 14th century, but afterwards the castle subsides almost into obscurity, a forgotten relic of an incredible episode in hisory. It saw some action in the Civil War, but afterwards was left to the elements.

No visit to Conwy is complete without a circuit of the town walls. They are one of the finest and most complete sets in Europe, over ¼ mile in length with 21 towers and three original gateways. There are excellent views from the section near the Upper Gate, and the remarkable group of 12 latrines adjacent to Mill Gate is quite unique.

In E part of town. C.   Bb4

A view across the outer ward at Conwy.

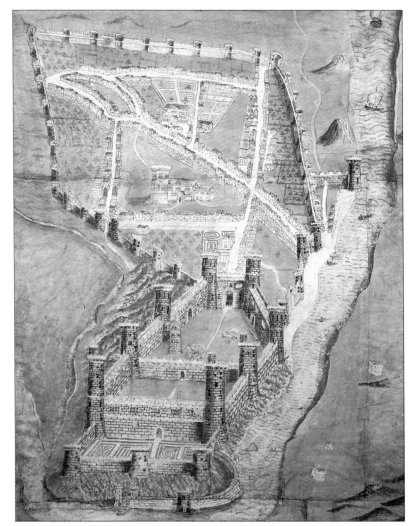

Conwy in about 1600, from a contemporary drawing in the possession of the marquess of Salisbury.

CASTLE AND TOWN

Castles were often the starting point — literally the foundation stones — of new towns that sprang up in their shadows. In early medieval times, the concepts of townships and town life were still alien to the Welsh. Then came the castles, bringing with them new commercial and trading opportunities and the first glimmers of an urban life as new communities grew up around their walls.

Early Norman towns — at Monmouth and Chepstow, for example — had their earth and timber defences and protective gates. In later times these were rebuilt in stone. Moreover, sophisticated, complete systems of defence were constructed, often part-and-parcel of total, purpose-built townships. This 'bastide' approach was first perfected in France, where defended towns were planned on a straightforward rectangular grid (reminiscent of today's American cities). Edward I was introduced to bastides during his expeditions in Gascony, subsequently applying the overall idea to his late 13th-century north Wales campaigns, where most of his new castles were built in tandem with fortified townships.

Castle and town became an integral unit with sturdy defensive walls extending from the immediate precincts of the fortress to encompass the entire community. Conwy's circuit of town walls is a particularly fine example of this approach, surviving complete for over three-quarters of a mile with 21 towers and three original gateways.

COSMESTON MEDIEVAL VILLAGE, NEAR PENARTH, SOUTH GLAMORGAN

Several years of hard work were recognized in 1986, when the Cosmeston medieval village project took first prize in the 'Heritage in Britain' section of the British Archaeological Awards. The Glamorgan-Gwent Archaeological Trust has been excavating the remains of a deserted village, and so far the work has unearthed 14th-century houses, farm buildings, a dovecot and an interesting kiln building.

The village took its name from the Norman Constantine family, but in the early 14th century the lands passed to the de Cavershams. Among other targets, the excavations have set out to see just why the village was eventually deserted. One of the most exciting aspects of the whole project, however, is the gradual creation of a 'living' site museum. Progress has already been made with reconstructing buildings, and experiments have been undertaken with medieval crops and even baking in a faggot oven. Further excavation and reconstruction is planned for future years.

On B4267 near Cosmeston Lakes Country Park 2m S of Penarth. C.   **Mb6**

One of the reconstructed medieval buildings at Cosmeston.

Criccieth Castle from the air.

CRICCIETH CASTLE, GWYNEDD

Perched high above the little seaside town, Criccieth crowns a rocky peninsula overlooking Tremadog Bay. From the top of the castle hill there are truly panoramic views, whereas the strategic value of this commanding position is immediately evident. In origin, Criccieth is a native castle of the Welsh princes, with three main building periods. Unfortunately, none of them is directly recorded, and scholars now disagree about who built what, so that it is impossible to be certain about its history.

Nevertheless, the hard core of the castle is the small but powerful inner ward, and this may well have been built around 1230-40 by Llywelyn the Great. Most impressive today is the twin-towered gatehouse, with three outward facing arrow-slits to each tower. This gate has no parallel among any of Llywelyn's other castles, but was perhaps copied from a contemporary construction at Beeston Castle in Cheshire. The entrance was protected by a portcullis and barred gate, with 'murder-holes' above. The towers provided domestic accommodation. Later in its history, perhaps under Edward I, the upper stage of the

Arrowslits in the gatehouse at Criccieth Castle.

gatehouse was raised at least once, as can be seen from the line of the filled-in battlements.

The next part of the castle to be built was probably the south-western section of the outer ward, with its simple gateway and large, rectangular tower. This work may date to the 1260s or 1270s, and probably belongs to Llywelyn the Last. Fine examples of decorated stonework were found in the large tower when it was excavated. It may have been of two or three storeys, and probably resembled the

keep at Dolwyddelan.

Criccieth fell to the forces of Edward I in 1283, and the king spent considerable sums in refortifying the castle. A further rectangular tower, the Engine Tower, was added to the northern end at this time and was linked to the remainder by stretches of curtain wall. Latrine shafts on its seaward side show that it was at least of two storeys. The name Engine Tower may well have been derived from the fact that it served to mount either a catapult, or a

larger stone-throwing machine — a grim reminder of the realities of warfare.

In 1295, in the Welsh rebellion under Madog ap Llywelyn, the coastal location of Criccieth proved its worth. During a siege of several months the English garrison was victualled by ship from Ireland, and found no great difficulty in holding out. Later in its history, under Edward the Black Prince, the castle had a notable Welsh constable. Sir Hywel ap Gruffudd had distinguished himself on the field of Crécy (1346) with the prince, and was known as 'Sir Howel of the Battle-axe'. By this time, the constable was probably accommodated in the south-east, or Leyburn Tower.

Criccieth's end came abruptly in 1404, with its capture by Owain Glyndŵr. The castle was sacked and burnt, never to rise again. The site now has an interesting exhibition on the theme of the castles of the native Welsh princes.

On hill overlooking town. C.   *Ad7*

CRICKHOWELL CASTLE, POWYS

Lying behind a main street in this pleasant, small country town are the ruins of one of the major castles of medieval Brycheiniog. On the right is the massive Norman motte, once surmounted by a circular shell keep — said by some to resemble the surviving example at Cardiff. At the bottom of the mound are the slight remains of a twin-towered gatehouse. The castle bailey forms a small playing field, and on one side is part of a large rectangular hall with a pair of towers, one round, and one square.

In town centre. F.   *Mb1*

THE CASTLES OF THE NATIVE WELSH

*W*hen mention is made of the castles of Wales, the mind invariably turns to those towering, all-powerful fortresses — such as Caernarfon, Conwy and Harlech — which survive as monuments to the ambitions of kings and the skills of the medieval military mason. Such is their presence that they eclipse another breed of castle, more accurately and authentically Welsh in that they were constructed by the native princes of Wales as opposed to the Norman invaders and those who followed in their footsteps.

Dolbadarn, Dolwyddelan, Castell y Bere, Castell Dinas Brân, Criccieth, Ewloe, Dinefwr and Dryslwyn are some of the castles that are truly Welsh. They are completely different in scale and concept to their mighty medieval contemporaries, in no way approaching the latters' force and strength.

Notable characteristics of the Welsh castles are their D-shaped and rectangular towers. More often than not, a tower will stand alone and keep-like, no more than two storeys high, surrounded by low, weak walls. This modest design betrays the reality of the disadvantaged situation in which the Welsh found themselves. The Welsh princes, for example, could never begin to match the spending power of the English crown. Moreover, most domestic buildings in Wales were of timber, not stone, so the Welsh nobility would have precious few indigenous stonemasons and skilled craftsmen at their disposal. Remember, too, that the native Welsh castles, built by princes who relied largely on bonds of kinship and loyalty, served an entirely different purpose to those put up by a monarchy intent on conquest.

The 'Picturesque' front elevation of Cyfarthfa — William Crawshay's 'baronial stronghold'.

CYFARTHFA CASTLE, MERTHYR TYDFIL, MID GLAMORGAN

In 1750 Merthyr Tydfil was no more than a village, yet by 1801 it had become the most populous place in Wales. Its phenomenal growth — as fast as any later American boom town — was due to iron. Powerful dynasties of ironmasters (Crawshays, Guests, Homfrays) controlled the four great ironworks at Cyfarthfa, Dowlais, Penydarren and Plymouth.

With slight regard for the primitive conditions of workers' housing, Cyfarthfa Castle was built for William Crawshay II as a romantic escape from the squalor and misery of his commercial and industrial life. Raised in a single year (1824–25), it has been called 'the most impressive monument of the Industrial Iron Age in southern Wales'. It was to overlook Crawshay's own ironworks (then the largest in Britain), and the exterior walls at least were grandly conceived in the new 'Picturesque' style. Avoiding the clean lines of Classical architecture, ruggedness is the essence of the design. The battlemented towers and false arrow-loops are a reminder of the medieval baronial past.

Today, the main suite of state rooms serves as a museum and art gallery. Here the visitor will notice that although the architect has continued the baronial theme to the entrance hall, there is a strong Classical influence in the style and comfort of the library, drawing room and dining room.

1m NW of town centre, off A470 (T). F.　　　　*Le2*

CYMER ABBEY, NEAR DOLGELLAU, GWYNEDD

The Cistercian abbey of Cymer was founded in 1198 and was colonized by monks from the mother house at Cwmhir, Powys. Its remote yet serene location, at the head of the Mawddach Estuary, is typical of the Cistercian order. It was destined to be a poor house, and suffered badly during the English wars of the 13th century.

Indeed, these wars were probably responsible for the failure to complete the original plan of the church. It lacks the usual transepts and presbytery at the east end, and thus has a simple rectangular, rather than a cross shape. The east wall, with its surviving tall lancet windows, was probably meant to be temporary, but in fact no more was ever built beyond. A *piscina,* or basin for washing the sacred vessels, can be seen at this end, and further west there are several sturdy octagonal arcade pillars. The tower at the far west was a 14th-century addition.

Little remains of the cloister to the south, though its layout has been preserved. The chapter house entrance can be identified to the east, and the monks' dining hall ran parallel to the church along the southern range. The drain here is not medieval. The little farmhouse to the west of the ruins almost certainly incorporates parts of the monastic guest house.

Cymer was dissolved in 1536 at which time its income was assessed at a little over £51.

1½m N of Dolgellau at Llanelltyd off A470(T) road. C.　　　*Dc3*

The thirteenth-century church at Cymer Abbey.

Denbigh Castle and town from the air.

DENBIGH CASTLE, CLWYD

When John Leland visited Denbigh in the mid 16th century, he commented that if the great gatehouse had remained complete it 'might have counted among the most memorable peaces of workys yn England'. The striking originality of this triple-towered construction reflects the architectural genius of its designer, James of St George, master of Edward I's building operations in north Wales.

The castle is located on the summit of what is a dramatically steep outcrop within the Vale of Clwyd. It was here that Llywelyn the Last's brother, Dafydd, had his chief stronghold, but of this no trace remains. Indeed, it was Dafydd's revolt in 1282 which led to King Edward's systematic annihilation of Welsh resistance in the north, and to the building of Denbigh Castle itself. The new lordship of Denbigh was granted to Henry de Lacy, earl of Lincoln, and the construction of the castle began almost immediately. The king, having started the work, left its completion in the hands of de Lacy. The southern and western walls were the first to go up, with their

projecting round towers similar to those at Conwy. The initial building of the town walls also belongs to this phase. The castle was taken by the Welsh during the revolt of Madog ap Llywelyn in 1294, and the remainder of the defences seem to date from after this episode. It is in the northern and eastern sections, including the gatehouse, that the work of Master James is most evident. The later curtain wall is much thicker, and the angular towers resemble those at Caernarfon. Most impressive of all is the superb gatehouse. Beyond its powerful defensive capabilities, it was embellished with chequered

stonework and probably a carved figure of Edward I above the entrance arch.

On the death of de Lacy in 1311, the castle may have been unfinished. There is a strong tradition that his eldest son, Edmund, fell into the well and died and that as a result the earl never completed the work. However, in the early 15th century it was held by Henry Percy, 'Hotspur', in support of Glyndŵr. During the Wars of the Roses, it was again the scene of warfare when in the 1460s Jasper Tudor launched two attacks against Yorkist defenders. During the Civil War it was held for King Charles, who stayed here for three days in 1645. He is believed to have lodged in the Great Kitchen Tower. Following a long siege in the following year, it surrendered to Parliament and redundancy.

In addition to the castle, there is much of interest to see in the town walls. The Burgess Gate to the north remains impressive, but the most dramatic remains are on the east, where a heavily-defended section includes Countess Tower and the slightly later Goblin Tower.

Overlooking the town from Denbigh hill. C.   Be5

Denbigh's great triple-towered gatehouse from the interior of the castle.

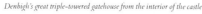

Dinefwr Castle, high on a hill above the River Tywi, is traditionally known as the royal palace of the princes of south Wales.

DINEFWR CASTLE, LLANDEILO, DYFED

At the end of the 12th century, Dinefwr was the seat of the powerful Lord Rhys, 'Prince of South Wales', and one of the most influential Welsh rulers during the reign of Henry II. Following the Battle of Bosworth, in 1485, Henry VII made a gift of the castle to Sir Rhys ap Thomas.

The ivy-clad silhouette stands at the edge of a river cliff, its defensive ditches cut from the solid rock. An early 13th-century round keep survives in the inner ward, as well as parts of the curtain wall. In the 15th century, a hall and solar were built on the side away from the cliff.

1m W of Llandeilo
Limited access, by pre-arranged tour during conservation work.   *Ke1*

DIN LLIGWY HUT GROUP, LLANALLGO, ISLE OF ANGLESEY, GWYNEDD

In its present form, this ancient 'village' probably belongs to the late Roman period, with 4th-century coins and pottery found here during excavations. The remains include two round stone huts, together with a series of rectangular buildings. The community was chiefly concerned with agriculture, though the excavations did reveal that some of the structures had been used for metalworking. The surrounding enclosure wall was probably intended to pen in animals, rather than provide any elaborate defence. Similar hut groups are found throughout north-west Wales, with origins extending back to the late Iron Age, or even earlier.

³/₄m N of Llanallgo Church off minor road. F.   *Ad2*

One of the round stone-built huts at the late Roman settlement of Din Lligwy.

DENBIGH FRIARY, CLWYD

This was a small house of Carmelite or 'white' friars, founded towards the end of the 13th century. The founder is not known for certain, but in the later Middle Ages it was patronized by the Salusburys of Lleweni. The greater part of the church survives, with the friars' choir to the east standing to roof level. A door to the south indicates access to the 'walking place' and formerly led from the cloister. The preaching nave to the west was for the lay congregation. Following its suppression in 1538 it was used as a dwelling, wool store and, finally, a malt house.

On eastern outskirts of town. F.   *Be5*

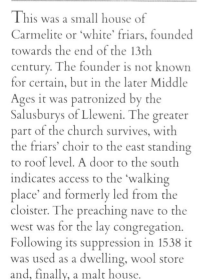

The entrance to one of the gold mines at Dolau Cothi.

though during the summer season there are guided tours which take in some of the underground workings.

Modern exploitation of the mines occurred from 1870-1910 and 1934-39. The site is now in the ownership and care of The National Trust.

Off the A482 at Pumpsaint. F. **Ga5**

The great seal [cast], 1205-06, of Llywelyn ab Iorwerth (By permission of the National Museum of Wales).

DOLAU COTHI ROMAN GOLD MINES, PUMPSAINT, DYFED

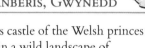

The Romans wasted no time in exploiting these gold reserves for the mines were worked shortly after the conquest of Wales around AD 80. As such, they represent the only site in Britain where we definitely know that the Romans mined for gold. The gold bullion was sent from here to the imperial mints of Lyons and, perhaps, Rome itself, and it has been suggested that its existence was one of the reasons why the Romans came to Britain. The aqueducts which served the reservoirs, tanks and sluices at Dolau Cothi appear as ledges on the hillsides, the 7-mile Cothi aqueduct running along the northern slope of Allt Cwmhenog.

The remains of opencast workings are overgrown, but some substantially preserve their Roman form. Galleries were driven through barren rock to the ore, and the horizontal entrances in the wooded slopes retain the marks of Roman chisels. Few shafts are accessible, however, and fences screen off dangerous parts of the mines,

DOLBADARN CASTLE, LLANBERIS, GWYNEDD

This castle of the Welsh princes lies in a wild landscape of breathtaking grandeur. The great tower still presides over Llyn Padarn, and from this precipitous location it commanded the entrance to the Llanberis Pass. Although nothing is heard of Dolbadarn before the conquest by Edward I, it seems certain that the builder was Llywelyn the Great, and that it was constructed to govern the ancient routeway from Caernarfon to the upper Conwy valley.

The earliest buildings, which may have included a hall, date from soon after 1200, but it is the circular tower which is the dominating feature. In contrast to the unmortared slate of the other structures, this was a well-built and fully developed round keep. It was probably copied by Llywelyn from similar towers built by his rivals in the southern March. Notice the once heavily barred first-floor entrance which, unusually, included a portcullis. The tower is traditionally the place where Owain Goch was imprisoned by his brother, Llywelyn the Last. A curtain wall surrounds the site, and there are traces of rectangular towers guarding the western and southern approaches.

½m SE of Llanberis F. **Ae4**

The round keep of Dolbadarn Castle overlooking Llyn Padarn.

DOLFORWYN CASTLE, ABERMULE, POWYS

Dolforwyn stands on a wooded hill overlooking the fertile Severn valley, a scene so peaceful today that it is hard to picture it as one of political animosity or military action. It was built between 1273-77 by Llywelyn the Last as a forward position in his territory, and overlooking the English lordship of Montgomery. Its initial construction led Edward I to write to Prince Llywelyn in 1273, forbidding him to build the castle. The prince replied, with a masterpiece of ironic politeness, that he did not require the king's permission to raise a stronghold in his own principality. Dolforwyn was, however, taken by Roger Mortimer after a fortnight's siege in 1277, and in the 14th century it gradually fell into decay and disuse.

The site has been the subject of archaeological attention since 1981, and to date details of a substantial 'square tower' have gradually been exposed on the south-western side of the ridge. A large courtyard lies to the north-east and, on the far side, a circular tower appears to be built into the curtain wall.

1m W of Abermule. Access via track off minor road F.   Eb6

DOLWYDDELAN CASTLE, GWYNEDD

At Dolwyddelan, a lonely square tower stands on an outlying ridge, looking out towards the rugged grandeur of Moel Siabod. A castle of the native Welsh princes, it continues to guard a landlocked mountain pass, once the medieval trackway from the Vale of Conwy to Ardudwy. Though written records have not survived, it was probably built about 1200 by Llywelyn ab Iorwerth. The tradition that this great Welsh prince was born here is unfounded, and there is a more likely location a little lower down the valley.

Nevertheless, Llywelyn's impressive keep is stern and functional. It was originally of two storeys but was modified in the late 1400s, and the battlements and wall-walks were reconstructed in the 19th century. A curtain wall surrounded the courtyard and a somewhat later tower lay to the west.

Dolwyddelan was a key to the native strategic defence of North Wales. When, in 1283, it fell to the English, Edward I promptly refortified the site to his own advantage.

1m from village and accessible by rough track off A470 C.   Ba6

DECLINE AND FALL?

By the late Middle Ages, castles were on the verge of obsolescence. Changes in society and fashion sounded their death knell, the final blow coming during the Civil War of 1642-48 when Parliamentarian guns caused irreparable damage to these medieval fortifications.

Further centuries of neglect and disuse — aided and abetted by builders who appreciated castle ruins only as a ready-made source of stone — did the rest. By the 18th and 19th centuries, overgrown ivy-covered ruins were, if nothing else, at least much favoured by artists and writers of the Romantic Movement.

Those with a cold, practical eye would have realized that these abandoned sites were in the final stages of decay. Today, they would be nothing but heaps of rubble had steps not been taken to renovate and preserve the ruins.

Of the hundred-odd castles in Wales now classified as 'visitable', many (including major showpiece sites such as Caernarfon and Harlech) are in the care of Cadw: Welsh Historic Monuments. One of Cadw's main responsibilities is the delicate, never-ending process of preservation. Most castles are roofless, their stonework exposed to the elements. Without constant maintenance, the rot soon sets in as joints loosen, walls start to crumble and nature begins, once again, to take hold.

Many other castles and country houses, in the ownership and care of local authorities, private owners and The National Trust, have benefited from similar measures.

The lonely castle of the Welsh princes at Dolwyddelan, guarding a major route through Snowdonia.

Dryslwyn Castle, set high above the River Tywi, was once the scene of a remarkable siege in the late thirteenth century.

DRYSLWYN CASTLE, NEAR LLANDEILO, DYFED

Originally built by the Welsh lords of Dryslwyn, the castle stands upon a steep hill commanding one of the few major crossings of the River Tywi. In 1287 it was the scene of a remarkable siege when the last Welsh lord, Rhys ap Maredudd, rose in revolt against Edward I. An army of more than 11,000 besieged Maredudd at the castle and it eventually fell, partly a result of the walls being undermined. Indeed, 150 men met a grisly end when an undermined wall fell upon them. Following the siege, Dryslwyn remained in royal control until at least the 15th century, though it was betrayed to Owain Glyndŵr in 1403.

Excavations since 1980 have begun to recover the plan and details of a fairly extensive stronghold. Work has been concentrated in the inner ward and the substantial walls of the hall and a round keep now lie bare. The outer ward lies along the ridge to the north-east. Adjacent to the northern side of the castle, the traces of the medieval township are clearly visible as humps and bumps in the turf.

On B4297 5m W of Llandeilo. F. Ke2

DYFFRYN ARDUDWY BURIAL CHAMBER, GWYNEDD

Situated on a hillside overlooking Cardigan Bay, this chambered tomb is of two periods of construction. About 3,500 BC a chamber was raised in the form archaeologists now call 'portal dolmen' type, with two portal stones either side of a high blocking slab. A capstone rested over these, and the whole

The magnificent stone chambers of Dyffryn Ardudwy – each represents a different phase in the history of the site.

was covered by a small and roughly circular cairn. Several generations later, a new larger chamber was constructed to the east of the first. A wedge-shaped cairn, about 100 ft long, was thrown up to cover this, and extended westwards to envelop the earlier tomb. Finds from excavations in 1961-62 included Neolithic and Bronze Age pottery. The absence of cremated bone suggests that the burials were inhumations.

Just off A496 at Dyffryn Ardudwy, 6m S of Harlech. F.   Da3

ELISEG'S PILLAR, NEAR LLANGOLLEN, CLWYD

Today, the remains of this 9th-century pillar cross carry just fragments of the original inscription. Fortunately, a copy of the text was made in 1696, and from this it is clear that there were once at least 31 lines recording the ancestry and ancient glories of the kings of Powys. The pillar perhaps rests on a prehistoric barrow and now stands some 8 ft, though its original height was probably close to 20 ft. It would have been of a type well known in parts of the English west Midlands, or the old kingdom of Mercia.

The inscription, of great interest, reveals that it was erected by Cyngen, last of the kings of Powys who died in 854, in memory of his great-grandfather Eliseg. It records that it was '*Eliseg who united the inheritance of Powys... out of the hand of the English with fire and sword*'. Further, the text claims the descent of the dynasty back to the Roman emperor Magnus Maximus. It was, however, normal for an early Welsh dynasty to legitimize its rule by claiming descent from some heroic figure. Magnus Maximus, the Macsen Wledig of the *Mabinogion*, was well suited to this role.

In field near A542 2m N of Llangollen. F.   Ec1

The ninth-century Pillar of Eliseg, near Valle Crucis Abbey, commemorates one of the early princes of Powys.

Erddig, where the 'upstairs – downstairs' arrangements of eighteenth- and nineteenth-century daily life are vividly displayed.

ERDDIG, NEAR WREXHAM, CLWYD

After being given to The National Trust in 1973, Erddig, a late 17th-century house, has been restored to its former glory, following 40 years of neglect and decay. It was built between 1684 and 1687 by Joshua Edisbury, and later refurbished in the early 18th century by John Meller, a prosperous London lawyer, who bought the house in 1716. On Meller's death in 1733, Erddig was left to his nephew Simon Yorke, the first of a direct line of Simon and Philip Yorkes who owned the house up until 1973, when Philip III gave the property with its 1,942 acres to The National Trust. Although the exterior of Erddig is no architectural masterpiece, the interior is beautifully furnished and has a collection of early 18th-century gilt and silvered furniture which is considered to be one of the finest and best documented collections in any country house. Erddig's domestic offices are equally fascinating, for they vividly illuminate the other, often ignored, ingredient within an 18th-century squire's house — the life and work of the domestic staff.

By seeing both sides of a country house, visitors come away with a rare insight into the 'upstairs, downstairs' arrangements, though Erddig is perhaps not entirely typical in this respect. The Yorkes were particularly good to their staff — they kept portraits of them; and composed poetic descriptions, now displayed in the Servants' Hall, which today help the visitor fully appreciate life at Erddig in its heyday. Amongst the range of outbuildings which have been restored are the laundry, sawmill, smithy and working bakehouse. The gardens, too, have been carefully restored to their 18th-century formal state. The Erddig Country Park Visitor Centre is located on the site of the former village of Felin Puleston.

Off A483, 1m S of Wrexham. C. Cc7

The cooking range in the kitchen at Erddig.

The Welsh-built castle of Ewloe in a wooded hollow on the border of England and Wales.

EWENNY PRIORY, BRIDGEND, MID GLAMORGAN

The priory was founded in 1141 by Maurice de Londres as a cell of the Benedictine abbey of Gloucester (now the Cathedral). The site appears to have been fortified from a very early stage, though this was probably for prestige rather than pure defence. Impressive walls, with gates remodelled about 1300, can be seen today. The austere eastern arm of the priory church, including the chancel and transepts, represents some of the finest surviving Norman work in Glamorgan. The south transept houses the founder's tomb. The nave, with its massive circular piers, still serves as the parish church.

*1½m S of Bridgend,
½m off B4524. F.*   Ld5

The tomb-slab of Maurice de Londres, founder of Ewenny Priory.

EWLOE CASTLE, NEAR HAWARDEN, CLWYD

Ewloe, a little-known castle of the native Welsh princes of Gwynedd, lies hidden in a wooded hollow, in what appears a most unlikely place for a castle. A visit, however, is well rewarded. Lying in the borderland, its walls remind us of the frequent clashes between the English and Welsh.

The characteristically Welsh D-shaped tower was probably built about 1210 by Llywelyn the Great. It was entered at first-floor level by means of an external stair, and served as a keep. The curtain walls and the circular tower to the west were added by Llywelyn the Last around 1257.

1m NW of Hawarden. F.   Cc5

FLINT CASTLE, CLWYD

Flint was the first of the castles begun by Edward I during his wars against Llywelyn ap Gruffudd, and his eventual conquest of north Wales. Construction commenced in July 1277, and by the end of August there were some 2,300 diggers at work. As with King Edward's other foundations in north Wales, the castle was attached to a completely new town established for English settlers. Building operations were

A manuscript illustration showing Richard II meeting Henry Bolingbroke in the inner ward of Flint Castle (By permission of the British Library, Harleian Ms. 1391, f.50)

Flint was one of the first castles to be constructed by King Edward I, during his campaigns to conquer Wales.

supervised by Master James of St George, though Flint is regarded as his most unusual commission for Edward I. The castle was substantially complete by 1284.

The inner ward is a strongly-built square, with a round tower at each corner. The whole is dominated by the great tower, or *donjon*, in the south-east corner. The entire castle was originally encircled by water. The great tower, however, was free-standing, with its own moat, and connected to the remainder by a drawbridge.

The castle played little part in the later Middle Ages, but is perhaps best known for its role in the events at the end of Richard II's reign. It was here that the king finally awaited the arrival of Henry Bolingbroke, hearing mass in the chapel on the upper floor of the great tower. The scene is immortalized in Shakespeare's *Richard II*, where the inner ward is described as 'the base court, where kings grow base'. From Flint, King Richard was taken to London, where the deed of abdication was signed. Bolingbroke thus succeeded to the throne as Henry IV.

Near town centre. C.   **Cb4**

Much of the surviving remains at Grosmont were built by Hubert de Burgh early in the thirteenth century, though the castle was later modified by the house of Lancaster.

GROSMONT CASTLE, GWENT

Together with Skenfrith and White Castle, Grosmont was one of the 'Three Castles' of northern Gwent, originally built by the Normans to control the major routeways between Herefordshire and the Usk valley. The earliest castle was constructed of earth and timber. Indeed, the name is derived from the French *gros mont*, 'big hill', which aptly describes the great earthen mound on which the later buildings stand. In 1201, King John granted the 'Three Castles' to Hubert de Burgh, and he was responsible for much of the work surviving at Grosmont today.

The rectangular two-storey hall block was probably built between 1201-04. The ground floor served as a basement with the main rooms, approached by an external timber staircase, on the first floor. In 1204 de Burgh was fighting for the king in France, and in the following year he became a prisoner of war. He did not regain his possessions until 1219, but soon afterwards, as at Skenfrith, Hubert began reconstructing Grosmont in an up-to-date style. Following French and English developments, a stone curtain was added, with a gatehouse and circular towers projecting out at the angles.

Henry III was in residence at Grosmont in 1233. He had come to suppress a rising in the Marches, but was forced to flee following a daring night attack by Richard de Clare. In 1267, the 'Three Castles' passed to the earls of Lancaster, and during the 14th century Grosmont was remodelled to provide apartments suitable for a noble household. In particular, the north-west block, distinguished by the tall chimney, represents changes at this time.

In 1404 the castle was besieged by the forces of Owain Glyndŵr. The Welsh were, however, defeated by a relieving force sent by Prince Henry, later Henry V.

On B4347, 10m NW of Monmouth. F.   **Hd7**

HARLECH CASTLE, GWYNEDD

As if its spectacular situation, foreboding might, and great power were not sufficient to ensure the fame of this magnificent castle, Harlech is also inseparably linked in Welsh myth with the tragic heroine Branwen, the daughter of Llŷr, of the *Mabinogion.* Mythology aside, it is small wonder that this is one of the most familiar strongholds in Britain. Seen from the bluff of rock to the south of the town, the view of castle, sea and mountain panorama is truly breathtaking. But not only has it an unsurpassed natural setting; as a piece of castle-building Harlech is also unrivalled. Even after seven centuries, it remains a testament to a military architect of genius, Master James of St George. Here he adapted the natural strength of the site to the defensive requirements of the age, and created a building which combines a marvellous sense of majesty with great beauty of line and form.

Harlech was begun during King Edward I's second campaign in north Wales. It was part of an 'iron ring' of castles surrounding the coastal fringes of Snowdonia, eventually stretching from Flint

The reverse of the great seal of King Edward I (By permission of the British Library).

Edward I's magnificent castle at Harlech.

around to Aberystwyth; a ring intended to prevent the region from ever again becoming a focal point of insurrection and a last bastion of resistance. Following the fall of the Welsh stronghold of Castell y Bere, King Edward's forces arrived at Harlech in April 1283, and building work began almost immediately. Over the next six years an army of masons, quarriers, labourers, and other craftsmen were busily engaged in construction. In 1286, with work at its height, nearly 950 men were employed under the superintendence of Master James. The final result was a perfectly 'concentric' castle, where one line of defences is enclosed by another. Unfortunately, the outer wall is ruinous today and fails to convey the true 13th-century effect.

provided the main private accommodation at Harlech. The first floor must have been for the constable, or governor, who from 1290-93 was none other than Master James himself. The comfortable rooms on the top floor probably served as a suite for visiting dignitaries, including the king.

The inner ward is surprisingly small and, as the foundations show, a great deal of room was originally taken up by the surrounding ranges of domestic buildings. To the rear lay the great hall and kitchen. Against the north wall were a chapel and bakehouse, and to the south a granary and a second hall. The corner towers provided further accommodation, and today the visitor may care to climb one of the sets of steps up to the wall-walks from which there are superb views in all directions.

The castle's other remarkable feature is the defended 'Way from the Sea', a gated and fortified stairway plunging almost 200 ft down to the foot of the castle rock. Once, this gave access to supplies from the sea, but the tide level has since receded, leaving Harlech somewhat isolated upon its rock. During Madog ap Llywelyn's uprising of 1294-95, this maritime lifeline proved the saviour of the garrison, which was supplied and victualled by ships from Ireland.

Harlech Castle played a key role in the national uprising led by Owain Glyndŵr. After a long siege, it fell to his forces in 1404. The castle became Glyndŵr's residence and headquarters, and one of the two places to which he is believed to have summoned parliaments of his supporters. It was only after a further long siege in 1408 that Harlech was retaken by English forces under Harry of Monmouth, later Henry V.

Sixty years later, during the Wars of the Roses, the castle was held for the Lancastrians until taken by Lord Herbert of Raglan for the Yorkist side. It was this prolonged siege which traditionally gave rise to the song *Men of Harlech*.

Near centre of town. C.   *Ae7*

The outer gate and gatehouse at Harlech. The upper floors of the great gatehouse provided the main private accommodation whilst below, the gate-passage contained an awesome display of deterrents to the would-be attacker.

The natural strength of the castle rock and cliff face meant that only the east face was open to possible attack. Here the gatehouse still offers an insolent display of power. The gate-passage itself was protected by a succession of no less than seven obstacles, including three portcullises. On either side of the passage were guardrooms, and the upper floors of the gatehouse

Haverfordwest Castle looms above the old bridge crossing the River Cleddau, dominating the centre of the town.

HAVERFORDWEST CASTLE, DYFED

From its high vantage point, the castle is a striking landmark which shows how excellent use was made of natural defences in a strategically important area. It was reputedly founded in the mid 12th century by Gilbert de Clare, earl of Pembroke and a powerful figure in the land, who had an eye for a strategic site. From this rocky hill 80 ft above the River Cleddau, his men could see for miles across the surrounding countryside, and the steep slopes were enough to daunt even the bravest attackers. Only to the south-west were artificial defences thought necessary, and here a deep ditch was dug. Parts of the Norman walls remain and inside there are remnants of a well, deep cut through the rock, but now filled in. All the castle masonry is extremely strong, and the curtain wall is 12ft thick on the north-west side.

A fourteenth-century seal from Haverfordwest (By permission of the National Museum of Wales).

The builders of the castle found an abundant supply of local material, and made full use of it. The walls are made of the type of gritstone known as Boulston, which was quarried just below the town on the river banks. Nolton sandstone has also been used extensively, especially for the window dressings. Two round towers, a chapel, hall, dungeon and parts of curtain wall remain on the hilltop, sharing the site with a large museum (once a prison).

The castle's ruinous state is due, largely, to the usual story — the battering it received during and after the Civil War, Cromwell ordering its destruction.

In centre of town. F. Jc5

HAVERFORDWEST PRIORY, DYFED

The priory lies on the west bank of the River Cleddau, a little way south of the medieval town. It was founded for Augustinian (black) canons, probably towards the end of the 12th century, by a member of the Tancard family, lords of Haverford. Unfortunately, little is known of its internal history, though the canons appear to have drawn much of their wealth from tithes in a number of surrounding parishes. At its dissolution in 1536, the priory was assessed to have a net income of just over £133.

Since 1983, the site has been under systematic excavation and is gradually yielding many of its long-hidden secrets. So far, the 13th-century east end of the church has been revealed, including the site of the high altar. The transepts and crossing have also been exposed, and work has extended to the chapter house and cloister to the south. The finds have proved of great interest, and include a fine selection of floor tiles and sculptured stone. Fragments of an effigy of a knight in chainmail were found in the chapter house, together with an extraordinary corbel with seven faces carved upon the front. Much more awaits discovery below the turf to the south of the church.

Located on W bank of the River Cleddau just S of town. F. Jc5

HAWARDEN OLD CASTLE, CLWYD

It was inevitable that a castle should be built on the first high ground one reaches in Wales after crossing the border from Chester. The original Norman earthwork motte made good use of the Iron Age hillfort built here in much earlier times. After the first earth-and-timber defences had proven vulnerable to Welsh attacks, Edward I ordered a stone fortress to be built about 1280 with a cylindrical tower 40 ft high. A fair portion of the keep survives, and two fine Early English windows in the curtain show the position of the hall.

In park just SE of town centre. C. Cc5

HAY CASTLE, HAY-ON-WYE, POWYS

Hay has had a stormy history. The castle was attacked in 1215, and later defences were probably attributable to the Norman lord, Humphrey de Bohun, in the latter part of the 13th century. The castle passed to the

One of over twenty circular stone huts forming an ancient farming settlement on Holyhead Mountain.

luckless dukes of Buckingham in the 15th century, the family adding Hay's square tower near the medieval gateway. Little remains of the castle, which fell into disuse after Edward, third duke of Buckingham, was beheaded by Henry VIII. The site is now dominated by a large, late-Tudor mansion, currently under restoration.

In town centre. Viewing from surrounding area only. Hb5

HOLYHEAD MOUNTAIN HUT CIRCLES, ISLE OF ANGLESEY, GWYNEDD

Scattered over the foot slopes of Holyhead Mountain, about 20 unenclosed circular hut foundations represent the remains of a once much larger settlement with up to 50 buildings. These stone-built structures, some with elaborate entrances, originally carried conical roofs of thatch or turf. Within several it is still possible to see traces of internal furniture such as benches and basins of stone. Small rectangular buildings can also be identified here and there in the group.

It seems certain that the huts formed part of an agricultural settlement during the Romano-British centuries. However, recent excavations have indicated that their origins may go back much earlier. A series of individual farms, surrounded by fields, could well have had a prolonged history extending back several thousand years to the Neolithic period.

On foot slopes of Holyhead Mountain. F. Aa2

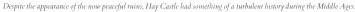

Despite the appearance of the now peaceful ruins, Hay Castle had something of a turbulent history during the Middle Ages.

KIDWELLY CASTLE, DYFED

Kidwelly is a remarkably complete and well preserved castle, with powerful defences going back to the early years of the 12th century. Established in the reign of Henry I, it bore the oppressive stamp of Norman control over south-west Wales. The mighty Bishop Roger of Salisbury raised the initial stronghold soon after 1106. Situated on a prominent ridge overlooking the River Gwendraeth, it could be supplied by sea, and formed part of a chain of new castles controlling a major coastal route.

Roger made use of the steep river scarp for the eastern defences, whilst he threw up a huge crescent-shaped bank on the exposed western flank. The bank was probably crowned by a timber palisade, and there must have been a substantial wooden gatehouse. It is interesting to note that the shape of the later medieval castle was to be heavily influenced by Roger's original plan.

By the 13th century Kidwelly had passed to the de Chaworth family and, following several damaging attacks by the Welsh,

Kidwelly was much altered over the medieval period, with the addition of finer accommodation and stronger defences. This aerial view of the castle shows how crowded the interior gradually became.

during the 1270s Payn de Chaworth set about rebuilding the castle in stone. The inner ward, with its four round towers, was squeezed into the existing enclosure. This was entered by simple archways on the north and south, each protected by a portcullis. The towers provided domestic accommodation, though only that on the south-west corner has stone vaults and floors.

The marriage of the de Chaworth heiress to Henry of Lancaster resulted in further alterations. Kidwelly was regarded as a great prize, and was now brought right up to date as a 'concentric' castle, with a 'walls within walls' arrangement. A new hall block was added to the inner ward, and a chapel, one of the perennial delights of this monument, was constructed in a new tower extending out over the river scarp. But the greatest development to the overall plan was the replacement of the outer timber defences by a stone curtain wall, with mural towers projecting into the ditch. A small gatehouse at the north end was overshadowed by a massive twin-towered example at the south. The most imposing feature at the castle, it contained guardrooms, a dungeon, a private hall, and other domestic accommodation for the constable. The gate-passage itself was protected by a drawbridge, a portcullis at either end, and 'murder-holes' above. Notice the three arches above the front entrance, through which rocks and other missiles could be dropped on attackers.

Around 1500, it was probably Sir Rhys ap Thomas who added further buildings to Kidwelly. The medieval castle could not provide the comforts expected in the Tudor age, and a new hall, kitchen and other lodgings were constructed in the inner and outer wards. By the early 17th century, however, the site had become 'utterly ruyned and decayed'.

As well as the castle, Roger of Salisbury was responsible for establishing the medieval town at Kidwelly. This was eventually defended with stone walls, and the early 14th-century south gate still survives.

Near town centre. C. Kc3

Kidwelly – one of the finest and most well preserved castles in Wales.

LAMPHEY BISHOP'S PALACE, NEAR PEMBROKE, DYFED

Lamphey Bishop's Palace – where the bishops of St Davids could combine the life of a prelate with that of a country gentleman.

By 1326, Lamphey had become the favourite residence of the bishops of St Davids, and little wonder. The magnificent buildings still speak for themselves, but a document of that year provides further insights into a lush country residence, with fishponds, orchards plump with fruit, well-stocked vegetable gardens, and a park of 144 acres. The palace had become a peaceful rural retreat, far from diocesan and secular affairs, where the bishop could combine the life of a prelate with that of a 'country gentleman'.

A large and well-appointed *camera*, or private apartment, was added to the early 13th-century hall, possibly by Bishop Richard Carew (1256-80). It was situated on the first floor, and was approached by an external stair at the front. Lamphey, however, bears the unmistakable imprint of Bishop Henry de Gower (1328-47), who was also responsible for sumptuous building at the bishop's palace, St Davids. He built a new and larger hall, a resplendent first-floor chamber over 70ft long. He also remodelled the courtyard, enclosing it with a battlemented wall. Moreover, the lofty arcaded parapets are typical of de Gower's work both here and at St Davids. At Lamphey, though, the workmanship is simpler, and possibly reflects the use of less skilled masons. Some further work of notable quality was executed in the early 16th century, probably by Bishop Edward Vaughan (1509-22). A chapel was added on the north side of the old hall, again on the first floor, and this has a particularly fine east window.

Under Henry VIII, the palace and rich manor passed to the Crown, and the king granted them to the Devereux family. Robert, later earl of Essex, and favourite of Elizabeth I, spent much of his boyhood here.

2½m E of Pembroke. C.　　　*Jd6*

Lamphey Palace from the air.

LAUGHARNE CASTLE, DYFED

Laugharne is perhaps best known for its associations with Dylan Thomas, but for the past fifteen years the picturesque castle, sited on the Taf estuary, has been the subject of painstaking archaeological investigation and gradual consolidation. There was probably a Norman castle here by the early 12th century, though the upstanding remains can be traced back no further than the work of the de Brian family in the late 13th century. From the de Brians and their descendants, in 1488, the lordship and castle passed to the earls of Northumberland. In 1584, Elizabeth I granted Laugharne to Sir John Perrott, said to have been the bastard son of Henry VIII.

The outer ward has a large diamond-shaped curtain wall, with a gatehouse on the north side. Within the inner ward, the two large round towers and part of the

Laugharne Castle — overlooking the peaceful waters of the Taf estuary.

inner gatehouse represent the de Brian castle. A hall block, which still stands between the two towers, was added in the Tudor period. However, as at nearby Carew, under Sir John Perrott, Laugharne was converted into a veritable mansion with a second hall constructed against the south curtain. Only the outer wall remains, but this reveals evidence of fireplaces and grand windows. The excavations have recovered much detail on the internal arrangement of both the Tudor and earlier buildings.

During the Civil War, Laugharne was captured by Royalists in 1644, but was quickly re-taken by besieging Roundheads. The castle was partially destroyed soon afterwards and gradually fell into decay. Its ivy-clad beauty was captured in a memorable painting by Turner.

On A4066 14m SW of Carmarthen At time of writing, closed for restoration, viewing from exterior only.   **Kb3**

LLANCAIACH FAWR HOUSE, NEAR GELLIGAER, MID GLAMORGAN

Situated in the Glamorganshire uplands, this superb gentry house has an atmosphere and character all of its own. The lofty proportions, massive walls, and the lack of large windows on the ground floor, all combine to give Llancaiach Fawr an air of medieval fortification. In fact, it was built in the early 16th century, almost certainly by David Prichard, whose family was descended from the Welsh lords of Senghenydd. The house survived, little altered until the early 17th century when various structural changes were made for greater convenience and a more impressive overall effect. After all, a Prichard served as sheriff of the county in both 1600 and in 1638.

Until recently Llancaiach Fawr was in danger of falling into a state of neglect and decay. Fortunately it has now been rescued by the local district council, and is gradually undergoing complete restoration. The house has three main floors, but there are also attics and there is a cellar below the rear wing. One of

the most interesting features is that the principal accommodation — the hall and parlour — is situated on the first floor, a tradition which can be traced back to some of the earliest Norman constructions in south Wales. There are many other early characteristics, including a remarkable number of mural staircases. It is also noteworthy that, as originally built, the medieval concept of a defensible home had not yet been discarded. All the ground-floor windows, for example, were barred, and the eastern part of the house formed a self-contained unit which could be closed off from the rest.

The early 17th-century alterations added a little more comfort and grandeur to Llancaiach Fawr. A spacious stair to the hall replaced the cramped originals, and panelling was introduced to several rooms. This work may have been contemporary with a cast-iron fireback in the parlour, which bears the date 1628 and the initials of David Prichard.

1½m W of Gelligaer, off B4254 Limited access during restoration work at time of writing.   **Ma3**

Llandaff Cathedral, Cardiff, South Glamorgan

Tucked away in a quiet corner of Cardiff's west side, near the banks of the River Taff, is the tapering spire of the solid stone cathedral of St Teilo, on a site which has witnessed Christian worship for over 14 centuries. The first stone cathedral did not rise here till the time of the Norman bishop, Urban (1107-33). Very little of his work remains though there is a fine arch behind the present high altar which is of Norman origin.

In 1220 the cathedral's west front was built, one of the finest pieces of medieval stone work in Wales. That it remains standing at all is one of the miracles of architecture: parts of the cathedral had been used as an ale house by Oliver Cromwell's troops, as a post office, one pinnacle crashed to the ground in 1703, a tower collapsed in 1723, and in 1941 German bombers destroyed the nave. All has now been restored to its former glory and has been further embellished by the erection of a fine organ loft in the form of a

The west towers at Llandaff Cathedral.

concrete arch supporting a striking sculpture of Christ in Majesty by Jacob Epstein, a modernistic representation which caused much controversy when first unveiled. Other recent additions include the building of a simple memorial chapel for the Welch Regiment and, on the outside walls, a series of carved stone heads representing the English monarchy, complete with crowns — except Edward VIII who

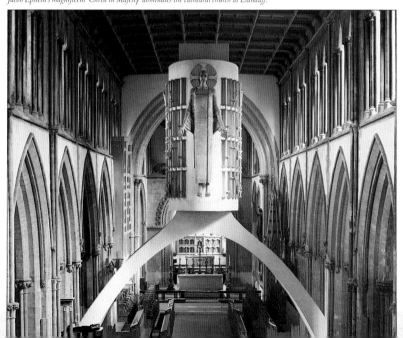

Jacob Epstein's magnificent 'Christ in Majesty' dominates the cathedral church at Llandaff.

was never crowned. Nearby, at the top of the steep path down to the cathedral's west front, are the remains of an ancient gatehouse; just across the road, in the ruins of the 800 year old bishop's palace — a public garden has been created which has won a Civic Trust award.

2m W of city centre in Llandaff. F.   **Ma5**

Llanmelin Wood Hillfort, near Caerwent, Gwent

During the last 500 years BC, Wales appears to have been divided into several main tribal areas, with the south-east eventually becoming the province of the *Silures*. In all parts of the country, settlements were almost universally defended at this time and, as elsewhere, the *Silurian* sites show signs of increasing strength as the centuries progress. Llanmelin is one such settlement, or hillfort, and occupies the top of a spur of Wentwood, overlooking the coastal levels of Gwent.

At first, the site may have been defended with a single bank and ditch, but these were replaced about 150 BC when the strongly-ramparted double defence was laid out. Inside, the settlement would probably have been densely occupied with circular wooden huts and storage buildings. An annexe to the south-east may have served as stock enclosures. At Llanmelin, as at other hillforts in southern England and Wales, the Roman legions met firm resistance. However, following the conquest, in the later 1st century AD they were gradually abandoned in favour of the new Romanized towns and settlements on lower ground.

7m W of Chepstow off the A48 (T) road. F.   **Me4**

Llansteffan Castle, Dyfed

While never one of the greatest of Welsh castles, Llansteffan provides the visitor with fascinating insights into the development of medieval fortifications. It stands on an abrupt headland overlooking the sandy Tywi estuary, on a site of great antiquity. Long before the castle was built, this bluff formed an Iron Age promontory fort, occupied as far back as the 6th century BC. It was refortified as an Anglo-Norman stronghold in the early 12th century, when the Iron Age ditches were recut and a 'ringwork' castle of earth and timber constructed within.

From the end of the 12th century until 1338 the castle was held by the de Camvilles, who were responsible for the successive stages of stone fortification. The square tower, or gate, in the upper ward was built about 1225, and stands on a slightly earlier curtain wall. An early 13th-century round tower has also been excavated on the line of the ringwork defences. The defences of the lower ward, with their impressive D-shaped towers, were added under the threat of Welsh assaults in the years after 1257. The north tower would have provided comfortable accommodation for the lord. Llansteffan's most imposing feature, however, is the massive twin-towered gatehouse, built around 1280. It was to become the main living quarters at the castle, and was later converted to a Tudor house. Originally, the gate-passage was protected by portcullises, and gruesome 'murder-holes' above. A slot-shaped chute over the front arch could be used to pour boiling liquids on attackers. The design of the gatehouse copies many features found at Caerphilly Castle.

The castle passed through various hands in the later 14th and 15th centuries, and some alterations were made under Jasper Tudor. It eventually sank into obscurity and became occupied by farm buildings.

On headland 8m SW of Carmarthen. F.   *Kb3*

The ruins of Llansteffan Castle occupy the former site of an Iron Age hillfort that once dominated the rocky headland above the Tywi estuary.

Llanthony Priory is set deep in the heart of the beautiful Black Mountains.

LLANTHONY PRIORY, GWENT

Gerald of Wales, himself no friend of monks or canons, contemplating Llanthony towards the end of the 12th century, recognized there '*a religious site truly suited to the monastic life...in a wilderness far removed from the bustle of mankind*'. Few could deny the great beauty of these ruins, blending so well with the rugged grandeur of the Black Mountains. The romantic scene echoes the very foundation, for it was here that William, a knight of Hugh de Lacy, stumbled upon a ruined chapel and resolved to abandon his profession of arms and establish a hermitage. He was joined by a priest, Ernisius, and by 1118 the infant community had become a monastery of Augustinian canons. The priory was to achieve considerable wealth and importance, but became a target of Welsh uprisings and many of the canons were forced to flee. In 1136, a new priory was founded on the

outskirts of Gloucester, and by the later Middle Ages this was to overshadow its remote mother house. However, as well as estates in south-east Wales, Llanthony was to draw a comfortable income from property in Ireland. It was suppressed in 1539, when there were just 4 canons with their prior in residence.

Recent archaeological excavations have revealed something of the complex building history at the site. An early 12th-century church was replaced between 1175-1220 by the upstanding construction. The north arcade of the nave is particularly lovely, and there are remains of the central tower over the crossing. In the 14th century the north transept was blocked off and converted to domestic use, with a kitchen, chamber and even a privy! The courtyard in front of the modern hotel preserves the form of the medieval cloisters, and the unusual 13th-century chapter house is on

the east side. The hotel occupies much of the west range. Further south, the present parish church formed part of the canons' infirmary.

On B4423, 6m NW of Llanfihangel Crucorney off A465. F.　　　Hc6

A glimpse of Offa's Dyke and the border into England is afforded by the arches of the ruined nave at Llanthony.

LLANTWIT MAJOR CHRISTIAN MEMORIAL STONES, LLANTWIT MAJOR, SOUTH GLAMORGAN

A fascinating collection of early Celtic crosses and medieval inscribed stones stands within the older part of Llantwit Major's imposing, cathedral-like church. The two oldest stones date from the 9th-10th centuries; both bear intricate carvings. The cross of Samson commemorates a local king of that name about whom nothing is known. Part of the inscription reads in translation: 'Samson set up this high cross for his soul'. A slab cross with carved wheel-head is believed to be a memorial to Hywel ap Rhys, king of Glywysing — the region between the Rivers Tawe and Usk — in the 9th century. It was probably the work of an Irish-trained sculptor.

Within Llantwit Major's church. F.　　　**Ld6**

The magnificent carved stone crosses, housed in the church at Llantwit Major.

Llanvihangel Court, though modified by time and circumstance, it still retains the atmosphere of a charming family home.

LLANVIHANGEL COURT, NEAR ABERGAVENNY, GWENT

In origin, this extremely fine house probably began as a late medieval hall. It was the seat of a manor held under the lordship of Abergavenny, and by the mid 16th century was in the hands of Rhys Morgan. The remodelling of Llanvihangel Court may well have been begun about this time, since its present appearance owes more to the standards of comfort required by the lesser gentry of the Tudor and Stuart periods. Situated within easy reach of the Black Mountains and the glorious Honddu valley, the house has many pleasing and memorable features.

The plaster ceilings and oak panelling are especially fine. But the exceptional feature is the beautiful 17th-century staircase, a typical Renaissance addition to such houses. The portraits and period furniture add to the interest of what very much remains a charming family home.

In village of Llanvihangel Crucorney, 5m N of Abergavenny. C.　　**Mc1**

LLAWHADEN CASTLE, DYFED

When Gerald of Wales visited his uncle, Bishop David fitz Gerald, at Llawhaden about 1175, he described it as a castle. It was already a site of great importance to the bishops of St Davids, and lay at the centre of some of their richest estates. Standing on a commanding spur above the Eastern Cleddau, in finely wooded country, the great oval ditch survives from the early stronghold visited by Gerald. In 1192, however, the defences were largely destroyed during a Welsh uprising. Following its recovery by the bishops, Llawhaden may have been rebuilt in stone during the 13th century, but it was not until the beginning of the 14th century that the castle was reconstructed on its present lines as the work of Bishop David Martin (1293-1328). As such, the former stronghold was transformed into an impressive fortified mansion, designed to provide the residence of a wealthy prelate, quarters for a permanent garrison and lodging for important guests.

The front of the gatehouse, added in the later 14th century, stands to its full height. Within, the buildings are set around a pentagonal courtyard. On the north-east, the two-storeyed block contained the great hall at the centre, with the bishop's private apartments in the east wing. The chapel and guest accommodation were ranged along the south-eastern side, with quarters for a garrison of mercenaries to the immediate west of the gatehouse.

Llawhaden was much used by the bishops for more than 250 years, though in the 16th century it was very largely abandoned in favour of a new palace at Abergwili near Carmarthen.

Llawhaden Castle – a fortified residence of the bishops of St Davids.

10m E of Haverfordwest off A40 (T) road. C. Jd4

LLIGWY BURIAL CHAMBER, LLANALLGO, ISLE OF ANGLESEY, GWYNEDD

The massive capstone of some 28 tons is one of the largest in Britain, and was supported by 8 squat uprights. The tomb seems to have been raised over a natural fissure in the rock, and a pit was dug beneath the capstone to form an 'underground' vault. Excavations

The massive capstone dwarfs Lligwy burial chamber giving it a low, squat appearance.

in 1908 revealed the bones of between 15 and 30 people of all ages. The discovery of Neolithic and early Bronze Age pottery underlines the protracted use of such tombs from their construction by the 'first farmers', through to the period of earliest metalworking.

³/₄m N of Llanallgo Church off minor road. F. Ad2

LOUGHOR CASTLE, WEST GLAMORGAN

The earthen 'ringwork' of the Norman castle at Loughor was thrown up over the south-east turret, and highest point, of the Roman fort of *Leucarum*. The oval enclosure overlooked a fording point on the Loughor estuary, and afforded protection to an infant borough established here in the

The scanty remains of Loughor Castle.

early years of the 12th century. The castle was burnt by the Welsh in 1151, but about 1220 it was given to John de Braose, the son-in-law of Llywelyn ab Iorwerth. Fragments of the curtain wall, probably built by de Braose, can be seen with further foundations just under the turf. The single surviving tower, which may have served as a keep, appears to be of slightly later 13th century date.

A twelfth-century tripod pitcher found at Loughor Castle (By permission of the National Museum of Wales).

On western edge of town near bridge. F. Ke4

MAEN ACHWYFAN CROSS, WHITFORD, CLWYD

Maen Achwyfan is a tall sculptured cross, the circular head of which resembles the shape of a wheel. Probably set up in the late 10th century, it is likely to commemorate a particular person or an event. The monument is carved on all four faces with interlacing, together with crude human and animal figures. It is clearly derived from Viking art styles, and represents the period when these sea raiders ruled the Irish Sea province, including north Wales.

In field near crossroads 1m W of village. F. Be4

MANORBIER CASTLE, DYFED

This captivating castle, overlooking the beach at peaceful Manorbier, is famous for its links with Giraldus Cambrensis, Gerald of Wales, who was born here in about 1146. Gerald, a prolific writer, called Manorbier *'the most delightful part of Pembroch...the pleasantest spot in Wales'*. The castle, mellowed by time, is probably a good deal more pleasant now than it was then, when it was a symbol of the hold which the Normans had on this corner of south-west Wales. It is noted for its particularly fine state of preservation, due to the durability of the local limestone from which it was built.

The first fortifications here were simple earthworks crowned by wooden buildings, but during the 12th century the stone castle of the powerful de Barri family began to take shape and building continued intermittently up to about 1300. When the baronial hall in the inner ward was excavated last century, an ecclesiastical gold ring came to light. Prisoners' quarters and fireplaces with ovens and tall chimneys were also discovered. On either side of the baronial hall are state apartments, where important guests were lavishly entertained. More humbly, the kitchens were on the north side of the inner ward near a well 30ft deep.

Giraldus, a scholar-priest with a fine turn of phrase, tells us that in his day the castle was *'excellently well defended by turrets and bulwarks'* and much endures despite the depredations of the centuries. Note the towers linked by high curtain walls and the strong gatehouse, which was one of the later developments. Remember, too, that in medieval times this was not simply a stronghold but a nobleman's seat which stood for gracious living. There was a huge fishpond to the north and a beautiful park with a vineyard at one end (the climate was gentler then!) and a grove of hazel trees at the other. A church and a mill were also within easy reach.

5m SW of Tenby. C.　　　　*Jd6*

A modern statue of Gerald of Wales by Henry Poole. Gerald was born at Manorbier in 1146 (By courtesy of Cardiff City Council).

Manorbier Castle in that 'most delightful part of Pembroke'.

The imposing entrance to Margam Abbey which survives from the Norman period, despite renovations in the last century.

MARGAM ABBEY, WEST GLAMORGAN

This was a centre of Christian worship more than 1,000 years ago, when monks of the Celtic Church had a monastery here. Their timber or wattle buildings were swept away when Robert the Consul, Norman earl of Gloucester, granted the land to Cistercian monks from the French abbey of Clairvaux for the founding of a daughter house. The abbey took 40 years to build and was the largest and wealthiest in Wales in the 12th century. The exterior was extensively altered during renovations last century, but the deeply-recessed doorway, flanked by banded shafts carrying carved capitals, belongs to the late Norman period around 1175–80. So do the three round-headed windows above.

The present parish church was formerly the monastic nave. Inside the church, the massive piers which divide the building into six bays have the simplicity and dignity of Norman work at its best. Those with an eye for detail may spot the bar-holes either side of the doorway, which enabled a stout oak beam to be thrust home to keep out intruders. The church was originally 272 ft long but is now only 115 ft, two bays at the east end having been cut off at the time of the Dissolution of the Monasteries in the 16th century. The south aisle contains tombs of the Mansels, the family who acquired Margam in the 16th century, and the west windows are the work of William Morris, Victorian artist, writer, and visionary.

The nearby Margam Stones Museum contains superbly sculptured wheel-crosses belonging to the early Christian period. The great cross of Cynfelyn, with its heavy base, is the most elaborate and may have commemorated an event rather than a person. Other stones include a Roman milestone which was turned into a Christian memorial and two 6th-century pillar stones, one of which is notable for its inscriptions in Ogham, an Irish influence which was felt in Wales at this time.

¼m off Junction 38 of M4 motorway. Abbey F; Museum C. Lc5

A fine collection of early Christian sculptured crosses can be seen in the Margam Stones Museum.

Margam Orangery – built to house Thomas Mansel's collection of citrus trees – still contains orange trees today.

MARGAM ORANGERY, WEST GLAMORGAN

The grandeur and scale of the Margam Orangery made it an irresistible attraction for the 18th- and 19th-century's important visitors to Wales. Designed by Anthony Keck, the orangery (1790) is simply a grand greenhouse, but it rivals many a palace in the perfect symmetry and scale of its architecture. It was built to house Thomas Mansel Talbot's collection of orange, lemon and citrus trees (about 100 in all). Some 327 ft long, with pleasing rounded arch windows letting in the light, the building is set off by an ornamental pond with fountain. Though most of the big houses of England and Wales once had their orangery, Margam is one of the few that retains its original function, with the orange trees standing in terracotta pots on coloured gravel arranged in a chequered pattern. It stands within the beautifully landscaped Margam Country Park, a testament to the wealth of the Mansel and Talbot families.

¼m off Junction 38 of M4 Motorway. C.   *Lc5*

MONMOUTH CASTLE AND GREAT CASTLE HOUSE, GWENT

King Henry V, born at Monmouth in 1387 (By kind permission of the National Portrait Gallery).

Monmouth is perhaps best known as the birthplace, in 1387, of the future King Henry V, victor of Agincourt, and Shakespeare's 'Harry Monmouth'. The castle was originally established by William fitz Osbern, one of William the Conqueror's most trusted barons, and was built to command an important double crossing of the Wye and Monnow rivers. An infant borough grew up around the castle and Benedictine priory, and the western approaches were eventually strengthened in the later Middle Ages by the gate tower which still survives on the Monnow bridge.

The oldest surviving building is the 12th-century hall-keep or tower, situated on the west side, and similar to that built by fitz Osbern at Chepstow. The hall was on the first floor, but was replaced about 1270 by a new building set at right-angles; probably this was the work of Edmund, earl of Lancaster. On the north is Great Castle House, built in 1673 by Henry Somerset, later the duke of Beaufort, to replace Raglan as his family's residence in the county following the Civil War. In 1875 the house became the headquarters of the Royal Monmouthsire Royal Engineer's (Militia), and as such it remains one of the few British castles still in military occupation.

On western edge of town. View castle from parade ground only. F.   *Me1*

The gate tower, which strides the Monnow Bridge, was built to strengthen the defence of the western approaches to Monmouth.

MONTGOMERY CASTLE, POWYS

Looking down from a high rock ridge above the small border town, the castle ruins stand guard over the Severn valley as it enters the Welsh hills. Montgomery was built by the young Henry III as a front-line fortress between 1223-34, and replaced an earlier earth and timber castle at nearby Hen Domen. Rock cut ditches divide the ridge into a series of wards, and it is the inner ward which comprises the stone stronghold of King Henry. The twin-towered gatehouse is one of the earliest of its type in Britain, and there is a well over 200 ft deep.

With the conquest of independent Wales by Edward I, Montgomery lost its role as a military spearhead. In the 14th century it belonged to the Mortimers, earls of March. Their additions, such as the bakehouse and brewhouse, were domestic and manorial rather than military or defensive.

In the 1620s Lord Herbert of Chirbury built one of the first brick houses in Wales in the middle ward. He played no part in the Civil War, but in 1644 the castle was seized by Roundheads. A Royalist siege under Lord Byron, in an effort to recover it, resulted in the battle of Montgomery; a crushing defeat for the Royalist cause. After the war, in 1649, the castle was demolished by order of Parliament.

Reached by Castle Hill. F.   Ec6

MURIAU'R GWYDDELOD, NEAR HARLECH, GWYNEDD

The name 'Irishmen's Walls' harks back to the belief that people of Irish extraction once lived in north-west Wales. They are, in fact, Iron Age hut circles with well preserved walls about 4 ft high and 18 ft thick, laid out on a hillside terrace. The cairns scattered about the adjoining fields are unlikely to be proof of further settlements, but probably came from this site.

In hills 1m S of Harlech. F.   Da3

NANTEOS, NEAR ABERYSTWYTH, DYFED

Nanteos is an historic house with a difference. Founded in 1739, essentially a country mansion of the Georgian period, this is no immaculately restored showpiece. The ultimate aim of the house's dedicated owners is full restoration — but they have some way to go yet. Visitors can thus gain a rare and illuminating insight into the realities involved in owning and preserving a substantial country home. Nanteos's former glory shines through in places. Its carved oak staircase, made from locally-grown timber, leads to an exquisite music room with an Italian

The finely restored music room at Nanteos, where composer Richard Wagner once stayed.

fireplace and fine plasterwork. The composer Richard Wagner stayed in this idyllically located house (Nanteos means 'brook of the nightingale'). For many years Nanteos was the home of a relic said to be the Holy Grail used in the Last Supper.

2½m SE of Aberystwyth off B4340. C.   Fe2

Nanteos is undergoing extensive renovation by its owners who intend to restore the splendours of this Georgian home.

NARBERTH CASTLE, DYFED

Once Narberth had five towers and a 'great deep dungeon', but it takes a lively imagination to picture this now. A fragment of wall shows the position of a window and door in the residential portion. It was the reputed site of the court of Pwyll, one of the legendary princes of the *Mabinogion*, a collection of early Welsh folk-tales.

At S end of town. C.   *Je5*

NEATH ABBEY, WEST GLAMORGAN

Alas, poor Neath, described by John Leland in the 16th century as 'the fairest abbey in all Wales', was forced to bear the scars of the Industrial Revolution. A 19th-century gentleman traveller was woefully to record that '*Neglected Neath, once the ornament of a lovely vale, looms up through its dense veil of smoke, like the skeleton of a stranded ship crumbling piecemeal to decay*'. Despite this, today it remains one of the most fascinating historic monuments in the Principality.

Essentially, the ruins are those of an abbey founded by Richard de Granville in 1130, established as a daughter house of Savigny in Normandy. In 1147 it was absorbed, with all other Savigniac monasteries, into the Cistercian order. Despite initial economic struggles, Neath became a fairly wealthy house, with extensive estates in Glamorgan, Devon and Somerset. Management and expansion of its Glamorgan estates led to a bitter dispute with the neighbouring abbey of Margam. The growing community soon outgrew the 12th-century buildings, and there were major programmes of reconstruction spanning the 13th and 14th

The Cistercian abbey of Neath, founded in 1130.

centuries. There are very complete remains of the west range, dating from 1170-1220, and originally occupied by the lay brothers who did much of the manual work on the abbey's estates. The superb 13th-century dormitory undercroft also survives. The abbey church was rebuilt on a grand scale between 1280-1330, and enough survives to illustrate the high quality of the architecture. In the south transept the night stair down from the monks' dormitory can still be seen.

The abbey was dissolved in 1539, and in 1542 passed to Sir Richard Williams, who was to give the site a new lease of life. It was probably Williams or his son who converted the south-eastern part of the cloister ranges into a grand mansion. It was skilfully

The remains of a sixteenth-century mansion raised over the monks' dormitory at Neath.

raised over the monks' dormitory and latrine, and is easily recognized today by the large rectangular windows of dressed stone. By 1600, the house and property had passed to Sir John Herbert, and was occupied throughout the 17th century.

Tiles from Neath Abbey depicting King Richard I and Saladin (By permission of the National Museum of Wales).

Copper smelting was introduced to the area in the 18th century, and this spread to the very precinct of this once proud abbey. Furnaces were set up in the west range, and workers were accommodated in lodgings carved from the abandoned Herbert mansion. The monastic kitchen was to become a casting workshop, and the entire site smothered in industrial waste. Encircled by canal and railway, it was not until the early part of this century that the site was gradually cleared of debris, in places up to 17 ft deep.

Off A48 ³/₄m W of Neath river bridge on Skewen Road. C.   **Lb3**

Newcastle – this may have been the work of King Henry II in the 1180s.

NEVERN CHURCHYARD CROSS, DYFED

This is one of the finest Celtic Crosses in Wales, dating from the late 10th/early 11th centuries. Historians know this as a 'free-standing composite pillar cross', and make sense of designs which to the layman are an intricate maze. The decorative treatment of the cross-head is similar to that found on later Scandinavian crosses in the Isle of Man. All four faces are embellished with carved patterns, and to the modern mind the skill and application involved is nothing short of astounding. The inscription on front and back remains a mystery.

7¹/₂m SW of Cardigan. F.   **Jd2**

NEWCASTLE CASTLE, BRIDGEND, MID GLAMORGAN

The 'new castle' on the banks of the Ogmore appears to have already existed by 1104, when it is first mentioned in a document. It is likely to have belonged to the Norman lords of Glamorgan. The stone defences, however, may well have been the work of King Henry II during a period when the castle was held in ward between 1183–89.

With its neighbours at Coity and Ogmore, Newcastle guarded crossings on the Ewenny and Ogmore rivers. The stone curtain wall and towers probably replaced an earlier earth and timber 'ringwork' castle. The south gateway includes some exceptional Romanesque architectural detail, especially for Wales. The rich carving certainly supports the notion of royal masons. Inside are the remains of a Norman hall, and there may have been a keep in the centre of the ward.

Near town centre on A4063. F.   **Ld5**

Nevern churchyard cross is one of the finest surviving early Christian monuments in Wales.

NEWCASTLE EMLYN CASTLE, DYFED

The time-worn remains of this castle, on a picturesque, grassy site overlooking a loop on the River Teifi, were once inhabited by, amongst others, Sir Rhys ap Thomas, friend of Henry VII. It would be hard to imagine a more serene setting for a castle than this, and one is not surprised to find it was intended as a country seat rather than a military post. Yet it had its share of excitement in the Civil War, when held for the king and blown up with gunpowder at the close of the struggle. There are remnants of some of the walls and the ruins of a gate. It is significant as the only native Welsh castle to be built in stone in this part of Wales.

On A484, 10m SE of Cardigan. F. Fb6

NEWPORT CASTLE, DYFED

When the Norman lords of Cemais chose this as the site of their new township in place of Castell Nanhyfer, the castle was erected on a circular mound probably surrounded by a moat. Dating mainly from the 13th century, its most substantial remains are those of the gateway and flanking tower, but there are also traces of an early English fireplace in the Hunters' Tower. The small medieval dungeon has an unusual herringbone ashlar lining.

S edge of town
In private ownership — viewing from
surrounding area only. *Jd2*

NEWPORT CASTLE, GWENT

On the muddy banks of the Usk, the castle replaced an earlier stronghold at the top of Stow Hill in the 14th century. The work was begun by Hugh, earl of Stafford. Following the Glyndŵr rebellion, it was reconstructed on grand lines by Humphrey Stafford, later duke of Buckingham. Three towers of this 15th-century work survive.

In centre of Newport, Gwent. F. Mc4

ST WOOLOS CATHEDRAL, NEWPORT, GWENT

In a town essentially bearing the marks of 19th-century industrialization, and perhaps more famous for its remarkable 'Transporter Bridge', St Woolos Cathedral is a precious remnant of Newport's medieval past. Even before the arrival of the Normans, a 'grave chapel' to St Gwynllyw — Woolos is a corruption of the name — may have stood on this ancient site at the top of Stow Hill. The church was acquired by the Benedictine abbey of St Peter at Gloucester, and the monks soon added the present nave to their new possession. In the 13th century the pre-Conquest structure (whatever its form) was rebuilt as St Mary's chapel, and this now survives as a western annexe to the Romanesque core of the cathedral. Throughout the Middle Ages St Woolos served as a parish church and this role continued until, with the creation

The west door and tower into Newport Cathedral.

The superb Norman arch in St Woolos Cathedral, Newport.

of the diocese of Monmouth, in 1921 it became the pro-cathedral, and in 1949 it achieved full cathedral status.

Visitors approach via the west door, where a sadly decayed and headless statue of Jasper Tudor — uncle of King Henry VII — stands in a niche of the 15th-century tower he reputedly built. Inside, the curiously sloping floor of St Mary's chapel possibly marks the site of Gwynllyw's shrine. At the east end of the chapel, the jewel of this little cathedral is the superb Norman archway into the 12th-century nave. Beyond, in the nave itself — the work of the Gloucester monks — the squat pillars with their bold capitals bear all the hallmarks of Norman architecture at its best. We can only guess at the appearance of the original aisles since, following extensive depredations during the Glyndŵr uprising, these were rebuilt in the 15th century.

To some, the chancel may represent something of a discordant note, though few can deny that it is visually striking. In 1960–62 the east end of the medieval church was demolished to make way for this more spacious chancel — the work of the architect A.D.R. Caroe. The mural and east window were designed by John Piper to complete the focal point of the new cathedral church.

¾m S of town centre at top of Stow Hill. F. Mc4

OGMORE CASTLE, MID GLAMORGAN

As the Normans advanced into Glamorgan during the closing years of the 11th century, the followers of Robert fitz Hamon may have been forced to halt for some while at the Ogmore river. Here, near the confluence with the smaller Ewenny, a castle was set up to guard an important bridgehead. The ruins of Ogmore Castle continue to overlook this fording place across the Ewenny, now marked by a picturesque series of stepping stones.

The earliest earth-and-timber castle took the form of a 'ringwork' and was probably thrown up by William de Londres ('of London'), who was certainly here by 1116. As at most important Norman castles in the area, Ogmore soon acquired a powerful stone keep. It is likely to be the work of William's son, Maurice, and the west wall still stands some 40ft high. There is evidence of a hall on the first floor, with two round-headed windows and a fine fireplace which represents a rare survival of the period. A third storey was added later as a private apartment of the lord. In the early 13th century, a stone curtain wall was erected on the line of the timber defences. A gateway was built next to the keep,

Ogmore Castle overlooks this ancient fording place across the Ewenny, still marked by a series of stepping stones.

and originally a drawbridge would have been located in front. On the other side of the keep, a turret was added projecting out over the ditch and housing two sets of latrines. A new hall eventually stood at the north end of the inner ward.

In the later 13th century Ogmore passed to the de Chaworths of Kidwelly, and eventually by marriage to the earls, later dukes, of Lancaster. The earthen defences of the outer ward were never replaced in stone. The remains of the 14th-century building in this area probably housed the manorial court, and represents the later medieval role of the castle as a centre of administration and justice for its lordship.

2½m SW of Bridgend on B4524. F.   *Lc6*

OXWICH CASTLE, WEST GLAMORGAN

The 'castle' here stands on a headland which forms the west side of Oxwich Bay. The extensive ruins are those of a sumptuous courtyard house built by the Mansel family during the 16th century, probably on the site of an earlier castle. A mock military gateway, bearing the arms of Sir Rice Mansel, leads to the former courtyard. Within, a southern block, occupied until this century as a farmhouse, represents Sir Rice's work of about 1520-38. The much larger eastern range seems to have been conceived as a single grand design, and dates to the ownership of Sir Edward

Picturesque Ogmore Castle was probably established by the de Londres family early in the twelfth century.

Part of the extensive ruins of Oxwich Castle — the lavish courtyard house built by the Mansel family.

Mansel, around 1559-80. The completed house represents the new and powerful Tudor gentry class in their element, living in the style of a past feudal magnate. The eastern range is of remarkable and complex design, with a first-floor hall and an elegant long gallery above. The surviving six storey tower-like block on the east, represents one of three vast projections on this side. They would have provided accommodation for the family, together with a multitude of retainers. Towards the north-east are the remains of a circular dovecot.

Off A4118, 11m SW of Swansea Closed to public during conservation work at time of writing. Viewing from adjacent footpath. **Kd5**

A medieval gold ring brooch found at Oxwich (By permission of the National Museum of Wales).

A grant of 1557 by Queen Mary to Sir Rice Mansel, allowing him to keep a personal retinue of fifty gentlemen (By courtesy of the National Library of Wales).

Oystermouth Castle, near Swansea, West Glamorgan

After the Welsh had burned down earlier Norman wooden castles on this site, the de Braose family — noted for their greed and lack of scruples — rebuilt this fortress in the later 13th century. After the subjugation of Wales, Edward I stayed there for two days in 1284.

Cromwell has been blamed for the destruction of the drum towers that flanked the gateway, but in fact the castle appears to have played no part in the Civil War. This may account for its exceptional state of preservation — the entire castle still stands to its original height, in an imposing position on a headland with wide views across Swansea Bay on the entrance to the Gower Peninsula.

Grooves for the wheels taking the chains of the drawbridge can be seen, and a modern copy of the original portcullis is in the entrance. A flight of stone steps beside the guardroom to the left of the entrance leads to a room with the romantic name of The White

The impressively complete remains of Oystermouth Castle still stand to their original height.

Lady's Chamber, but — white lady or no — the truth is that this was one of the governor's principal apartments. The keep is notable for its handsome apartments with beautiful windows. Those in the banqueting hall, in the northern half of the keep, are in Early English style. The adjacent chapel block also has fine early 14th century windows. An attractive combination of military and domestic influences, Oystermouth must have been one of the most desirable residences on Gower.

On A4067 at the Mumbles, 4m SW of Swansea. C.   La4

PARC LE BREOS BURIAL CHAMBER, NEAR SWANSEA, WEST GLAMORGAN

Situated on the narrow floor of a dry valley, this peaceful site has something of an eerie atmosphere, echoing the rituals of the distant Neolithic past. The tomb was constructed around 4,000–3,500 BC, and is of a form linked to the group which archaeologists call 'Cotswold-Severn', after the area in which they chiefly occur. The cairn is about 70ft long, with two rounded 'horns' at the southern end, flanking a funnel-shaped forecourt. This leads to the central passage which has two 'transeptal' chambers at either side. The capstones from these have long since disappeared. Excavations in 1869 and 1960-61 recovered the fragmentary remains of at least 25 Neolithic people buried in the tomb, though the figure may originally have been as many as 40.

¹/₂m NW of Parkmill, a village on A4118 approx 8m SW of Swansea. F.   Ke5

PEMBROKE CASTLE, DYFED

Pembroke Castle has kept up appearances remarkably well, but the grandeur of its outer fabric is deceptive — for within those lofty walls and keep, very little remains. The castle has a long and fascinating history, for it was around 1090 that Arnulf of Montgomery built the small inner bailey standing at the end of the promontory. Only a few years later the castle withstood a long siege by the Welsh, although its defenders were near starvation. The late 12th-century keep is both an outstanding feature and architectural novelty, for it has a massive cylindrical tower with an unusual stone dome. Views from the top are tremendous and the castle's natural defensive position on a rocky promontory overlooking Milford Haven is immediately apparent.

The main room on the second floor has two windows embellished externally by dog-tooth moulding and a carved head. All the rooms are circular and the keep is nearly 80 ft high. It was the work of

An aerial view of William Marshall's mighty Pembroke Castle.

William Marshall, son-in-law of Strongbow, conqueror of Ireland and the man responsible for the wholesale reconstruction of the castle in stone in the late 12th/early 13th centuries. Another absorbing feature of the castle is the gatehouse, which had a complex barbican and no fewer than three portcullises.

A battlemented flying arch inside the gatehouse is something of a puzzle, for it would appear to be of little use in repelling invaders who had actually forced entry into the castle. Still, the gatehouse is, overall, a mighty defence which proves the skill and the sophistication of military architects in medieval times. Pembroke is also noteworthy as the only castle in Britain to be built over a natural cavern, a large cave known as the Wogan.

Historically, Pembroke is important not only for its masonry but for the fact that Harri Tudur, who became Henry VII and inaugurated the Tudor line of monarchs, was born there in 1457 — reputedly in a room above the portcullis chamber.

During the troubled reign of King Charles I, the castle was attacked in turn by both Royalists and by Roundheads as the sympathies of its occupants altered. In the latter stages of the struggle an attacking force was led by Cromwell himself.

On NW edge of town. C.   *Jd6*

PENALLY CHURCH CROSS, PENALLY, DYFED

This highly decorated slab cross is interesting for its mixture of Celtic and Northumbrian influences. The wheelhead of this cross cannot be earlier than the 9th century and the free interlacement rings in the decoration are typical of the age of the Vikings, so it is likely that this free-standing cross dates from the first half of the 10th century. The beautifully wrought vine scroll is characteristically Northumbrian. All the faces are carved with patterns in low relief and the head and shaft of the cross are edged with thin cable mouldings. The cross-head is of Anglian type, with wide splayed arms.

2½m S of Tenby. F.   *Je6*

One of the keep tower rooms in Penhow Castle, finely restored to reflect its twelfth-century origins.

PENHOW CASTLE, NEAR NEWPORT, GWENT

A perfect example of the smaller type of fortified manor house, Penhow was developed from a heavily-built keep necessary to protect the knightly retainers of the local earl, who lived in almost impregnable majesty at nearby Chepstow Castle. In 800 years, buildings have developed higgledy-piggledy around the inner bailey, occupying almost every square inch of this small courtyard within the curtain-wall. Essentially, Penhow is made up of three successive houses ranged around a central courtyard — a medieval keep, 15th-century hall block, and opulent late Stuart house. The main buildings which can be seen by the public are the 12th-century keep tower with its ramparts, the 13th-century curtain wall, the lower hall of the 14th and 15th centuries, the dovecot, with its holes opening from the side of the building, and the Tudor wing. There is very little dating from after the building of the tree-shaded Restoration façade to the

The remarkable domed stone-tower of the keep still dominates Pembroke Castle today.

Today, the buildings which survive include the south range of the monastic cloister. A three-storey 13th-century block contained the canons' dining hall, with the dormitory above and a cellar at ground level. A two-storey extension at the east end dates to the 16th century, and may have housed a kitchen and 'warming house'.

Nearby, an impressive dovecot was built about 1600 by a local landowner. With its massive domed roof, it has room for nearly 1,000 birds.

The Augustinian priory at Penmon. The origins of this monastic site can be traced back to the sixth century.

main living quarters, which was designed to give the ensemble a more modern and less military aspect. Still in private ownership, Penhow claims to be Wales' oldest inhabited castle.

Just off A48 (T) road approx 6m E of Newport. C.   **Md4**

On eastern tip of island. F.   **Ae2**

PENNARD CASTLE, NEAR SWANSEA, WEST GLAMORGAN

Time and weather have left their mark on Pennard. Sand covers the courtyard, and on the windward side the greater part of the curtain wall has collapsed, although some repairs have been carried out since 1961. The gate towers are the most impressive features of Pennard's stumpy, sandy remains. It can never have been a favourite domicile, for the castle was abandoned by 1400, just over 100 years after its construction in stone. It is best viewed from the north, where the curtain wall is almost intact. The hall was typical of its kind, with a private room for the lord, twin service rooms and a principal room where a blazing fire burned in the hearth. The castle overlooks Three Cliffs Bay, one of the most scenic spots on Gower.

By footpath ½m S of Parkmill on A4118, approx 8m SW of Swansea. F.   **Ke5**

PENMON PRIORY, NEAR BEAUMARIS, ISLE OF ANGLESEY, GWYNEDD

This tranquil location on the eastern tip of Anglesey has remains spanning over 1,000 years. It was the site of a monastery dating back to the time of St Seiriol, who is believed to have lived in about the 6th century. A holy well which survives may have its origins in this period. In the early 13th century the Celtic community was reorganized under the Augustinian Rule, and at this time the priory church was enlarged. This now serves as the parish church.

Pennard's once mighty castle – now at the mercy of the ever-encroaching sand.

Penrhyn Castle – built in the neo-Norman style – is the splendid creation of Thomas Hopper for the slate baron, G.H. Dawkins Pennant.

PENRHYN CASTLE, BANGOR, GWYNEDD

Compared to the old mines and quarries, Penrhyn Castle is a very different reminder of north Wales' 19th-century slate industry. It was built by Thomas Hopper for G. H. Dawkins Pennant, who drew on the huge profits of the Penrhyn slate quarries for its construction. The resulting neo-Norman castle is regarded not only as Hopper's masterpiece, but the apogee of the Norman Revival in Britain. Dating from 1320-37, this sumptuously-appointed building is not a castle in the strict, historic sense for its architecture reflects an opulent rather than a combatant spirit.

Exterior and interior are both magnificent. The castle's location in grounds overlooking the Menai Strait complements a lavish, no-expense-spared interior. Look out for the use of slate throughout the house: entwined dolphin supports for the large side table in the Great Hall, a full-size billiard table in the library, even a bed (which weighs over a ton) in the principal bedroom, all painstakingly carved from slate. These are just some of the delights of this outstanding,

gigantic 'sham' castle, with its Great Hall, Drawing Room, Library, Ebony Room, Chapel, Dining Room, Bedrooms and Industrial Railway and Doll Museums.

Penrhyn, in the ownership and care of The National Trust, stands amongst attractive woodland and grounds that contain a Victorian walled garden.

*Off the A55 (T) just E
of Bangor. C.*   *Ae3*

PENTRE IFAN BURIAL CHAMBER, NEAR NEWPORT, DYFED

One of the most impressive megalithic monuments in Wales, this majestic burial chamber of the Neolithic period lies in foothills of the Preseli Mountains. Today, all that remains is a skeleton of a single oblong chamber, with a great capstone 16½ ft long supported by three uprights. A semicircular forecourt was originally defined by two large stones either side of the central 'portal'. The chamber lay at the southern end of a wedge-shaped cairn that must initially have been about 120 ft long. Built perhaps more than 5,500 years ago, the stones are all from the Preseli Mountains, which also provided the famous 'blue stones' at Stonehenge.

*3m SE of Newport on minor
road. F.*   *Je2*

The impressive megalithic remains of Pentre Ifan burial chamber.

Picton Castle, now much modified, probably owes its origins to Sir John Wogan, in the time of King Edward I.

PICTON CASTLE, NEAR HAVERFORDWEST, DYFED

A large motte at Slebach probably represents the original Norman castle in this area. Towards the end of the 13th century this was replaced — on a new site — by the powerful Edwardian castle which now survives as Picton. The core of the building, with its four round towers, was probably built by Sir John Wogan who was Justiciar of Ireland under King Edward I. From the Wogans Picton passed to the Dwnns, and in the later 15th century an heiress married into the Philipps family who continue to hold the castle today. Picton was besieged and taken by the forces of Glyndŵr in 1405, and was captured twice during the Civil War — first by the Royalists in 1643, then by Parliament in 1645.

A new four-storey block was added to the castle about 1800, with further additions some fifty years later. Since 1954 Picton has been extensively restored to serve as a modern residence.

The main apartments of the castle are open through much of the Summer, and the extensive gardens are an added attraction.

Picton also houses an art gallery with a fine collection of Graham Sutherland paintings.

On minor road, off A40 (T), 3½m SE of Haverfordwest. C.   Jd5

PLAS GLYN Y WEDDW, NEAR PWLLHELI, GWYNEDD

The present owners bought this Victorian house with the intention of reviving its former function — that of an art gallery. Plas Glyn y Weddw was originally completed in 1857 as a dower house for the Madryn estate. In 1896 it was purchased by Solomon Andrews, a prominent Cardiff businessman, and it was he who developed the building as an art gallery. Visitors could catch a tram from Pwllheli, and three afternoons a week bands played in the grounds of the house. Following a period of neglect, since 1979 the building has been restored, with contemporary paintings, ceramics and sculpture from all over Wales on exhibition.

Built in the Gothic style, the most distinctive feature of the house is the spacious entrance hall. Here, the effect of a somewhat grand staircase and elaborate timber roof is completed with the generous use of stained glass.

4m SW of Pwllheli, off A499. C. Ac7

PLAS MAWR, CONWY, GWYNEDD

This is another of Conwy's many architectural gems. The house ('Great Hall' in English) was built between 1577 and 1580 for Robert Wynne, an influential Welsh squire. A powerful, rugged exterior constructed from local grey stone contrasts with the superb ornamental plasterwork of the interior for which Plas Mawr is justifiably famous (look out for the frequent appearance of the initials 'R.W.').

The plasterwork shields and crests, now white, would originally have been tinted in correct heraldic colours, creating a blaze of splendour. They were either whitewashed after the Roundheads' capture of Conwy in 1646, or perhaps plastered over by the Royalists to preserve them from destruction.

The building itself, now the headquarters of the Royal Cambrian Academy of Art, is also worth examination. One of the turrets has been heightened, giving a magnificent view of the town. And, perhaps as a gesture to Father Time, you can count 365 windows and 52 steps leading to the watchtower. Rooms include Queen Elizabeth's Parlour (with the Queen's initials) and the Lantern or Haunted Room, associated with the inevitable grim legend.

In centre of town. C.   Bb4

Plas Mawr — 'the most complete memorial to Elizabethan Wales'.

The magnificent mansion of Plas Newydd is set beside the Menai Strait with superb views across to Snowdonia.

PLAS NEWYDD, LLANFAIR P.G., ISLE OF ANGLESEY

Given to The National Trust by the Marquess of Anglesey and opened to the public for the first time in 1976, Plas Newydd is a magnificent mansion in an unspoilt setting beside the Menai Strait. Extensive gardens and woodland, together with superb views of Snowdonia, add to the attractions of this site. Although meaning 'new place' in English, Plas Newydd's history stretches back almost 500 years. The present mansion, though, dates in the main from the late 18th century, when extensive alterations were undertaken.

The Georgian Gothic style employed by architect James Wyatt and his assistant Joseph Potter is evident immediately: on entering the park, the first building to be seen is the stable block with its pointed archways, spires and tracery.

These architects were also responsible for the Classical and Gothic interiors of the present main block. With so much to see inside this splendidly furnished and appointed mansion, it is superfluous to attempt a description here. Outstanding, though, are the Music Room and the Rex Whistler Room, decorated by the painter's largest mural (a 58 ft canvas, painted between 1936 and 1940, of an Italianate coastal scene). One quirky exhibit, on view in the house's Cavalry Museum, is the 'Anglesey leg', one of the world's first articulated artificial legs, used to replace the limb lost by the first marquess in the Battle of Waterloo.

Overlooking Menai Strait off A4080 1m SW of Llanfair P.G.. C.   Ad3

PLAS NEWYDD, LLANGOLLEN, CLWYD

Plas Newydd is a black-and-white timbered mansion, built in the striking 'magpie' style of the borderland, and decorated with a wealth of oak carvings. For 50 years it was the home of the so-called 'Ladies of Llangollen', Lady Eleanor Butler, the Hon. Sarah Ponsonby and their maid Mary Carryll (who rejoiced in the nickname 'Molly the Basher'). They fled the constraints of Irish country life to establish a highly eccentric — and much talked-about — household here from 1780, which attracted many famous figures of the time, including Shelley, Byron and Wordsworth.

SE of town centre. C.   Ec1

The eye-catching black-and-white timbered house of Plas Newydd was once the home of the famous 'Ladies of Llangollen'.

Plas Teg — virtually derelict until a short time ago — has now been elegantly restored.

PLAS TEG, NEAR HOPE, CLWYD

The recent history of this magnificent Jacobean house is nothing less than a huge success story. Only a few years ago, with the roof gaping and the interior open to the elements, Plas Teg — 'Fair Mansion' — was in a state of extreme neglect and in danger of complete dereliction. Now, in a miraculously short space of time, the house has been completely restored due to the efforts and single-minded determination of a remarkable new owner. Filled with beautiful objects and decorations, there is much to interest the visitor — not least an unusual collection of parrots and macaws!

The symmetrical lines and compact square plan betray the Renaissance origins of Plas Teg. It was probably completed about 1610 for Sir John Trevor, who held an important Admiralty post as Surveyor of the Queen's Ships. Such is the quality of the building, it seems likely a Court architect was involved. Sir John, like other 'new men' of his age, was anxious that his house would make a show on relatively restricted means. He could not afford the fashionable luxury of a courtyard house, but instead the central core of three storeys is surrounded by projecting towers at each corner. As such, the design reveals a hankering after the outward appearance of medieval military architecture.

Inside, the hall, great chamber, a host of bedrooms and bathrooms are all restored to their original splendour. The superb staircase — somewhat typical of so ambitious a Jacobean mansion — is particularly memorable. In fact, discovering the delights of Plas Teg today, we can be thankful for what so nearly might not have been.

2m N of Caergwrle on A541. C. Cc6

PLAS YN RHIW, NEAR ABERDARON, GWYNEDD

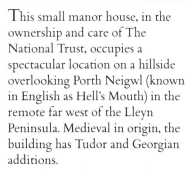

This small manor house, in the ownership and care of The National Trust, occupies a spectacular location on a hillside overlooking Porth Neigwl (known in English as Hell's Mouth) in the remote far west of the Lleyn Peninsula. Medieval in origin, the building has Tudor and Georgian additions.

Plas yn Rhiw's immediate surroundings are as intimate as the views are magnificent. The house stands amongst ornamental gardens and woodland, with a glorious profusion of rhododendron, azalea, yew, fir — even sub-tropical shrubs.

12m from Pwllheli on S coast road to Aberdaron. C. Aa5

POWIS CASTLE, WELSHPOOL, POWYS

Most of the great Welsh castles were allowed to decay when the medieval wars ended, but Powis survives as a captivating example of a military stronghold which was preserved and renewed by continued occupation. Its fabric contains architecture of many different periods, beginning with a medieval square keep and stone hall. The most fleeting glimpse of Powis' mellow red gritstone walls tells us that this stately country house is a place rich in history.

It was a seat of the princes of Upper Powys in the critical struggles of the 13th century, but in those days of disunity and intrigue they cast their lot with the English and were punished by the powerful Llywelyn the Last, who destroyed the previous castle in 1275. As the century drew to a close the local prince, Gruffudd ap Gwenwynwyn, was given a barony by Edward I on

The grand stately home of Powis Castle was once the seat of the medieval princes of Upper Powys.

condition that he dropped his princely title, and having agreed to this the family set out on a massive building programme which laid the foundations of the present castle. In Elizabethan times it came into the hands of Sir Edward Herbert, a younger son of the earl of Pembroke, who spent an enormous sum in refurnishing it. Powis fell to parliamentary troops in the Civil War but the castle escaped the fate of those strongholds Cromwell knocked about a bit. In the 18th century the formal gardens were laid out and their basic design has not altered since then. They are today perhaps the finest 'hanging' gardens to be found anywhere in Britain. The enormous clipped yews, with their rounded shapes, act as a remarkable 'architectural' foil to the strong lines of the castle's pinkish stonework.

The grand terraces, on which most of the garden beds are planted, look east to the Breidden Hills and fall gently away to the Severn Valley below. There is an orangery with 18th-century framed windows, surmounted with a balustrade bearing four lead figures of shepherds and shepherdesses.

Inside the house, there is a magnificent Baroque staircase, an Elizabethan Long Gallery and gilded State Bedchamber. The dining room has a carved Chippendale suite with scroll and pierced backs. A Charles II walnut settee and collection of family miniatures are in the library, and the original Elizabethan plasterwork in the Oak Dining Room can be seen in the west window aperture. There are Brussels tapestries of the late 17th century in the State Bedroom and the staircase murals are signed and dated by Lanscroon, 1705. The Clive of India Museum, recently opened in the Ballroom range, contains the collection of Indian art brought back by Lord Clive and his son in the 18th century. These are some of the treasures in one of Wales' most ancient and historic houses, now in the ownership and care of The National Trust.

1m S of town. C.   Ec5

An aerial view of the superb fifteenth-century castle at Raglan.

One of the many elegant rooms at Powis Castle.

RAGLAN CASTLE, GWENT

Raglan, stately and handsome, is perhaps deceptive. The might of its angular towers bears comparison with the great castles of Edward I, and suggests its origins lay in the bitter conflicts of the later 13th century. In fact it belongs mainly to the 15th century, and was as much a product of social aspiration as it was of military necessity.

It was begun by Sir William ap Thomas, a veteran of the French wars, who grew wealthy through exploiting his position as a local agent of the duke of York in south-east Wales. About 1435 he began building the Great Tower, subsequently known as 'the Yellow Tower of Gwent', probably on the site of a much earlier Norman motte and bailey castle. Surrounded

heraldic glass, and the roof was built of Irish oak. Earl William also added the long gallery, without which no great Elizabethan house was complete.

At the outbreak of the Civil War, Raglan was garrisoned for the king. Henry, the new earl, and later marquess of Worcester, poured his fortune into the royal cause. By 1646 the castle was under siege, one of the longest of the war. It was pounded by heavy artillery under the command of Sir Thomas Fairfax, and finally the elderly marquess was forced to surrender.

The fall of Raglan virtually marked the end of the Civil War, and Cromwell's demolition engineers were soon at work reducing the walls. However, the strength of the Great Tower was almost great enough to defy them. Only after 'tedious battering the top thereof with pickaxes', did they eventually undermine the walls and two of its six sides were brought crashing down in a mass of falling masonry.

Just off A40 (T), 7m SW of Monmouth. C.   *Md2*

William Herbert's great gatehouse at Raglan Castle.

by a water-filled moat, the unusual hexagonal plan of the tower, together with its elaborate drawbridge arrangements, are more easily paralleled in France than in England. Within, there was a single large room to each floor, and the entire structure echoed the power and influence of its builder.

Following ap Thomas's death, he was succeeded by his son William Herbert, who continued to develop Raglan. As a prominent Yorkist, he played a major role in securing the throne for Edward IV in 1461, and was raised to the peerage as Lord Herbert of Raglan. Eventually rising to earl of Pembroke, his political career is reflected in his sumptuous building. Under Herbert, Raglan became a veritable palace, unmatched in the 15th century southern March. He added the great gatehouse, the Pitched Stone

Court and also rebuilt the Fountain Court with a series of formal state apartments for himself and his household. All of these repay careful examination. Notice, for example, the circular gun ports in the lower part of the gatehouse. The great kitchen lay in the tower at the corner of Pitched Stone Court, and its huge ovens and fireplaces remain.

Herbert was beheaded following his defeat at the battle of Edgecote in 1469, and there were no further major alterations to Raglan until the ownership of William Somerset, earl of Worcester (1548-89). In the main, he was responsible for extensive changes to the hall, which remains the finest and most complete of all apartments in the castle. The huge fireplace survives, as does the tracery of the beautiful windows. These were once filled with

RHUDDLAN CASTLE AND TWTHILL, CLWYD

When Edward I ordered the construction of his new castle in 1277, Rhuddlan had long been a place of settlement. The site is now known to have been occupied by an Anglo-Saxon *burh*, named *Cledemutha*. By 1063 it was the Welsh princely seat of Gruffudd ap Llywelyn and, ten years later, Robert of Rhuddlan established an early Norman castle here. Robert's motte survives as a great earthern mound some 300 yards to the south of the later stronghold, and is known today as Twthill.

The Norman motte at Rhuddlan stands above the River Clwyd.

The new castle was begun as part of King Edward's first campaign against Llywelyn the Last. Work began on the construction late in 1277 and continued through until 1282. The initial task was to provide access from the sea, two miles away. This was a formidable task, and required major digging operations to create a new channel for the River Clwyd. Building at the castle was supervised by Master James of St George who followed a plan based upon 'concentric' lines, with two parallel lines of defence. The outer ward slopes down to the river, where there was a dock protected by Gillot's Tower, perhaps named after the mason

EARLY CASTLES

The popular vision of the castle — an image of grey curtain walls, battlemented towers, sturdy gatehouses — dates from the time when these strongholds were first built in stone. At Chepstow, work began on one of Britain's first stone-built castles soon after the battle of Hastings, around 1067-71. This was, however, virtually a unique exception.

The several hundred other castles thrown up during the earliest phases of the Norman conquest of Wales do not perhaps conform to the general picture of a medieval stronghold. Almost all were built of earth and timber, structures which Norman lords of all ranks could erect speedily and with the minimum of effort.

The most common form was the motte and bailey, with almost 250 sites known in the Principality. The 'motte' was an imposing mound, often about 20 to 30ft high, and defended by wooden fortifications. The 'bailey', a curved enclosure also defended by earth and timber, contained buildings such as the hall, chapel, kitchen and barns.

Another form of early castle, located chiefly in the south and west, is known as a 'ringwork'. Up to 80 examples are recorded, and in each case a bank and ditch enclose a roughly circular area, once entered by a stout timber gatehouse.

Various factors help to explain the differences, including chronology, personal preference, and, perhaps most important of all, the geological nature of the subsoil. Today, many mottes and ringworks can be easily identified at sites where the original earth and timber defences were replaced in stone. At Cardiff and White Castle the early mottes are still very clear, whereas at Kidwelly and Ogmore the later stone layouts were heavily influenced by the initial ringwork defences. Elsewhere in Wales, isolated, overgrown mounds or banks sometimes mark the site of long-abandoned Norman earthwork castles.

later found at Conwy. The diamond-shaped inner ward is quite symmetrical, having two massive twin-towered gatehouses, with single towers in the other two corners. Within the ward, the walls were originally lined by timber-framed buildings including the King's Hall, the Queen's Hall, the kitchens and the chapel. Traces of these can be seen in the beamholes and roof creasings cut in the curtain wall.

In 1284, the Great Statute of Wales, or the Statute of Rhuddlan as it is often known, was issued

Rhuddlan Castle — raised by King Edward I following his first campaign in Wales.

The Statute of Wales, 1284.

from the castle and has assured its place in history. As a settlement for the country, it survived until the Act of Union in 1536 when Wales was merged with England.

3m S of Rhyl on A525. C.   **Bd4**

The medieval castle at Ruthin is now a comfortable hotel.

RUTHIN CASTLE, CLWYD

Ruthin was built at the same time as Flint and Rhuddlan, during Edward I's campaigns against Wales in the late 13th century. As such, it benefited from the influence, and perhaps the hand, of Master James of St George, the architectural genius responsible for the great Edwardian castles of north Wales. Ruthin is situated on a ridge of red sandstone rising 100ft above the Clwyd. Its late 13th-century castle has seen extensive rebuilding over the centuries. Even though the restoration of the older parts of the castle is not entirely authoritative, the general picture is accurate enough. In the outer courtyard of the west wall, a house built around 1830 fills half of a rectangle 240 ft by 160 ft. Historically, the castle is forever associated with an episode that led to the Owain Glyndŵr uprising of the early 15th century.

Although lacking in technical interest the reconstructed castle is indeed an elegant building set in spacious and attractive gardens. Ruthin Castle has now been converted into a luxury hotel which serves as a particularly apt setting for medieval banquets. Both residents and non-residents are welcome to attend these evenings of traditional food, wine, mead and entertainment.

In town centre. Interior viewing by appointment only to non-residents of hotel.   **Ca6**

ST ASAPH CATHEDRAL, CLWYD

Originally founded about AD 560, modest St Asaph was refounded as a cathedral in 1143, as part of the Norman reorganization of the Welsh church. With a length of only 182 ft, it is just about the smallest cathedral church in Wales or England. Though it was much changed during a major restoration by Sir Gilbert Scott, 1867–75, the fabric of this dignified little building has much to interest the visitor.

The cathedral was largely rebuilt after it had been burned by Edward I's troops in 1282. The nave, transepts and crossing belong to the early 14th century, and the central tower was added in 1391–92. Inside, in the north aisle, is the mysterious 'Greyhound Stone' which has baffled heraldic experts. From the tower one of the best panoramic views of the lower Vale of Clwyd can be enjoyed. The cathedral's

St Asaph Cathedral, much restored in the nineteenth century.

museum displays a collection of stone and bronze artefacts, coins and a dictionary compiled by the 19th-century scholar-tramp, Dic Aberdaron. A memorial to Bishop William Morgan (1545-1604), the influential religious figure who first translated the Bible into Welsh, and produced other translations, stands in the cathedral precincts.

In the city on A525, 6m
S of Rhyl. F.   *Be4*

St Cadfan's Stone, Tywyn, Gwynedd

The narrow, 7 ft-high pillar of stone is of great historic importance, for its inscription is thought to be the oldest surviving record of the Welsh language. The 7th-century inscription reads, 'The body of Cingen lies beneath'; not entirely definitive, for more than one saint was called Cingen. The link with St Cadfan, founder of the monastery on Bardsey Island, is now reckoned more tenuous. This tall pillar-stone, once subject to the indignity of being used as a gatepost in a field, bears an inscription in Old Welsh on all four sides. The lettering is preceded by an incised linear Latin cross with barred upper terminals on the front and rear faces.

In St Cadfan's Church, Tywyn. F.Da5

St Davids Bishop's Palace, Dyfed

During the Middle Ages there were few landowners in Wales greater or wealthier than the bishops of St Davids. As well as being princes of the Church, they were Marcher lords in their own right, owing allegiance only to the king. It is hardly surprising, therefore, that at their cathedral city these powerful prelates created a group of medieval buildings unsurpassed anywhere west of Offa's Dyke. Even in ruin, the palace is a magnificent architectural splendour, speaking volumes of men rich in experience of both Church and State. The entire cathedral close was surrounded by a precinct wall and one of the four gates, 'Porth y Tŵr', which dates to about 1300 remains standing. Within, the palace is very largely the work of a succession of 'builder-bishops' who held the see in the later 13th and 14th centuries.

Edward I and his queen were at St Davids on pilgrimage in 1284, and their visit may well have called attention to the inadequacies of the early medieval palace. About this time, Bishop Thomas Bek (1280-93) began a programme of new building commensurate with his role as a major churchman and former statesman of King Edward. He was responsible for the chapel in the south-west corner, the hall and private apartments, and the gate. The bishop's hall and the private chamber were on the first floor, and were carried on a series of barrel vaults. Notice the superb

An aerial view of the bishop's palace and cathedral 'city' of St Davids.

series of corbels carved as human heads, from which sprang the main trusses of the roofs in this range.

But the man who more than any other left his imprint decisively and characteristically on this palace

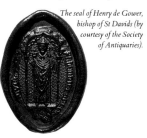

The seal of Henry de Gower, bishop of St Davids (by courtesy of the Society of Antiquaries).

was Bishop Henry de Gower (1328-47). In addition to major works in the cathedral itself, including the imposing rood screen, it was de Gower who built the Great Hall, which remains undoubtedly the finest range. Moreover, he brought a graceful unity to the palace with the distinctive arcaded parapet which takes command of the beholder's eye. It is similar to the bishop's other work at Lamphey, and probably Swansea. The hall is again on the first floor and was designed for the entertainment of important guests. The wheel window in the east gable is a sheer delight, and the majestic porch would have provided a fitting entrance to so fine a building. Notice, too, the chequered pattern in the stonework on the upper stages, which must have been very striking in its original colours.

Later bishops made further additions and alterations to the palace, but with the Reformation the story of decay and destruction in the 16th and 17th centuries begins.

A new exhibition, entitled *Lords of the Land,* is situated in parts of the palace undercroft. It tells more of the wealth and power of the medieval bishops, and explains the phases in the growth of the buildings.

Near centre of St David's. C.　　*Ja4*

St Davids Cathedral, dedicated to the national saint of Wales.

ST DAVIDS CATHEDRAL, DYFED

St Davids is one of the great historic shrines of Christendom. Nowhere in Britain is there a more ancient cathedral settlement, for it reaches back fourteen centuries and survived the plunder of the Norsemen in the 'Dark Ages'. St David chose this wild, beautiul region as the site of his monastery in the 6th century and you will find his shrine in the purple-stoned cathedral, which nestles inconspicuously in a grassy hollow beneath the rooftops of the tiny city.

The large, cruciform cathedral, dating from 1176, is a treasury of fine things. The nave has a breathtaking beauty, embodying three centuries of craftsmanship which now make up a scene of medieval splendour. There are superb examples of the woodcarver's art at St Davids — just gaze upwards at the decorative roof — and the choir stalls date from the late 15th century. Here, note the wit and zest of the medieval misericord carvings (carvings on the hinged seats in the choir stalls); they represent a trend away from the decorative severity of earlier times, and show that even in religion, humour had its part to play. A chapel dedicated to St David's mother, St Non, stands on a nearby headland.

Near centre of St David's. F.　　*Ja4*

The presbytery and high altar at St Davids Cathedral.

The Tironian abbey of St Dogmaels, founded about 1115.

St Dogmaels Abbey, near Cardigan, Dyfed

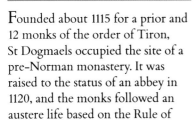

Founded about 1115 for a prior and 12 monks of the order of Tiron, St Dogmaels occupied the site of a pre-Norman monastery. It was raised to the status of an abbey in 1120, and the monks followed an austere life based on the Rule of St Benedict.

The surviving ruins span four centuries of monastic life and show much alteration. Parts of the church and cloister are 12th century. However, the west and north walls of the nave, which stand almost to their full height, are of the 13th century, and a fine north doorway has 14th-century ballflower ornament. The north transept is Tudor, retaining elaborate corbels which supported the stone vaulting. Notice here the carved figures with an angel representing St Matthew, a lion for St Mark and the Archangel Michael. The footings of the chapter house can be seen to the west of the cloister, with the adjacent monks' infirmary standing almost to roof level. At the Dissolution the church continued to be used for a time by the parish, and a rectory was built into the south-west corner of the cloister.

³⁄₄m W of Cardigan Bridge. F.   **Je1**

St Fagans Castle and Welsh Folk Museum, near Cardiff, South Glamorgan

St Fagans is a large Elizabethan mansion, built within the walls of an abandoned medieval castle. A clear Renaissance influence is apparent in the symmetrical elevation of the east front, though the internal planning recalls traditional elements. Many rooms in the house are still fully equipped with furniture and household bric-a-brac spanning many centuries. After a period of neglect, St Fagans was restored in the 19th century, and in 1947 the mansion and adjacent parklands were donated by the earl of Plymouth to the National Museum of Wales. It was to provide the focus for a Welsh Folk Museum, which today houses extensive collections illustrative of the material culture of Wales.

A second side to this fascinating site is the modern, purpose-built museum block standing close to the Elizabethan mansion. This covers themes such as religion, medicine, education, agriculture and music, with exhibits from lovespoons to harps, period costumes to kitchen utensils and hundreds of other homely items.

But for many, the high point of St Fagans is the third side. This is

One of the 'vernacular' buildings of Wales, rebuilt at the Welsh Folk Museum, St Fagans.

to be found in the surrounding grounds, where old 'vernacular' buildings brought from all parts of Wales have been lovingly and painstakingly re-erected, stone by stone, timber by timber. Amongst the buildings here are a woollen factory, several styles of farmhouse, a cottage, a row of early industrial cottages, a tannery, a tollgate house, a cockpit and even a pigsty. And in keeping with the image of a living museum, a wood turner and blacksmith are amongst the craftsmen working at the site, displaying traditional skills in producing items which were familiar in times gone by, thus helping to build up a complete picture of life in the rural Wales of old.

At St Fagans on W outskirts of Cardiff. C.   **Ma5**

The glorious Elizabethan great house of St Fagans.

ST LYTHANS BURIAL CHAMBER, NEAR CARDIFF, SOUTH GLAMORGAN

Situated close to the larger example at Tinkinswood (see separate entry), the chamber of this Neolithic tomb is now almost completely exposed. Three great upright slabs support a massive capstone, and there are traces of the original mound some 90ft long. Burial and ritual were taking place here probably more than 5,000 years ago.

The Neolithic chambered tomb at St Lythans.

½m S of St Nicholas, a village on A48 (T) just W of Cardiff. F.   Ma6

SEGONTIUM ROMAN FORT AND MUSEUM, CAERNARFON, GWYNEDD

The Roman fort of *Segontium* is one of the most famous in Britain. Its upstanding ruins assured it a place in legend as the *Caer aber Seint* ('the fort at the mouth of the Saint river') mentioned in *The Dream of Macsen Wledig*, one of the early Welsh tales of the *Mabinogion*. Today, it is the

An aerial view of the Roman fort of Segontium, with Edward I's Caernarfon Castle in the distance.

only site in Wales where it is possible to see something of the internal layout of a Roman auxiliary fort.

Segontium was established under the governor Agricola about AD 78, and was part of a network of forts constructed during the final crushing Roman offensive on Wales. It was intended to guard the Menai Strait, occupying a pivotal position in the new Roman road system. Unlike virtually all others, it was held more or less continuously until about AD 395, if not slightly later, and it must have served as a supply base for the whole north-west of Wales. The outline of the fort was of the usual 'playing-card' shape, covering almost 6 acres, and perhaps designed for a unit of up to 1,000 auxiliary troops. The original defences comprised a single earthen bank and ditch, with four timber gates. Inside, all of the buildings were of wood at this stage. Reconstruction in stone began in a

piecemeal fashion after about AD 140. The defences were finally completed in stone in the early 3rd century, when the water supply and internal buildings were also reconstructed. The 4th century again saw much renewal, especially after 369, and a great deal of that visible today dates from this later period.

At the centre of the fort lay the headquarters building. This had a courtyard, an assembly hall, with the regimental chapel to the rear where the standards of the unit were kept. In the 3rd century an underground strongroom was constructed beneath the chapel. To the west was the commandant's house, which had four ranges of rooms leading on to a small central courtyard. The free-standing platform in one of the rear rooms is almost certainly the base of a domestic shrine. The barracks lay to the north and south, and part of a granary can be seen near the north-east corner. South of the modern road, a footpath leads to the line of the south-western fort wall with its central gate. The gate itself had a pair of passages, flanked by towers, and a guardroom can be seen in that to the right. The wall originally stood some 17 ft high.

Traditionally, the garrison was removed finally by the rebel general Magnus Maximus, the Macsen Wledig of legend, in 383. But recent archaeological evidence has revealed that occupation at some level continued through to the end of the century. A well laid out museum at the site illustrates more of the history and buildings, and many of the finds discovered during excavations are on display. Segontium is owned by The National Trust in the guardianship of Cadw: Welsh Historic Monuments.

On Constantine Rd, leading from Pool St. F.　　　　*A d4*

SKENFRITH CASTLE, GWENT

Throughout the Middle Ages, Skenfrith was held in common ownership with its neighbouring strongholds at Grosmont and White Castle. Together, these 'Three Castles', as they became known, controlled the routes from England into Wales in the gap of fairly open country between the cliffs of the Wye valley and the Black Mountains to the north-west. Skenfrith stands on the Monnow, and the early Norman castle was no doubt intended to guard this important river crossing.

In 1201, as a reward for faithful service, King John granted the 'Three Castles' to Hubert de Burgh. He lost them in 1204, when he became a prisoner of war in France, and it was not until 1219 that de Burgh fully recovered his possessions. Subsequently, as Justiciar of England and earl of

An ivory chess piece found at Skenfrith Castle (By permission of the National Museum of Wales).

Kent, Hubert appears to have completely levelled the earth and timber castle at Skenfrith, and by 1232 had replaced it with an up-to-date stone construction. Much influenced by his years of warfare against Philip Augustus, king of France, de Burgh's new castle could not fail to echo contemporary French developments. The plan is dominated by the circular keep, standing at the centre of a rectangular ward with a round tower on each of the angles. The keep was originally entered at first-floor level, by way of an external timber stair. Within, a fireplace reveals that the second floor provided domestic accommodation. The top of the tower was probably surrounded by a projecting circular wooden gallery, or *hourd*, allowing archers to cover the ground on all sides of the castle. A bridge crossed the moat to the gatehouse on the north side. The corner towers have deep basements for storage, and their doors are raised above ground level for security. Against the western side of the court, a large rectangular range probably included a great hall, which may have been half-timbered.

In 1239 Hubert de Burgh surrendered the 'Three Castles' to Henry III, and they eventually passed to the earls of Lancaster. There were, however, no significant additions made to the fabric at Skenfrith.

On B4521, 11m NE of Abergavenny. F.　　　　*Md1*

Hubert de Burgh's Skenfrith Castle, set deep in the Gwent countryside.

STRATA FLORIDA ABBEY, PONTRHYDFENDIGAID, DYFED

In June 1164, the Norman baron Robert fitz Stephen drew a colony of 13 Cistercian monks from Whitland to found the abbey of Strata Florida on the banks of the Fflur. The abbey was a modest foundation, but its fortunes changed when the Lord Rhys ap Gruffudd overran fitz Stephen's estates. Rhys assumed the patronage of the monastery he 'loved and cherished', and by 1184 had begun to build the monks a church on a new site. They took possession of this in 1201, though building must have continued well into the 13th century.

Strata Florida, 'the Vale of Flowers', is a typical Cistercian site, located in the green and tranquil heart of Wales. The austerity of the order appealed to the Welsh, and

The early thirteenth-century west doorway at Strata Florida Abbey.

this house, in particular, became one of the centres of native culture and influence. In 1202 the monks secured a collection of books from the library of Gerald of Wales, and in 1238 the abbey was the scene where an assembly of Welsh princes swore allegiance to Llywelyn the Great's son, Dafydd. There is good reason to believe that part of the *Brut y Tywysogyon*, or Chronicle of the Princes, was written at Strata Florida, and many native rulers are believed to have been buried here. Indeed, in the 14th century, the greatest medieval Welsh poet, Dafydd ap Gwilym, was probably laid to rest within the precinct.

Huge upland estates provided pasture for extensive sheep farming, contributing much to the early wealth of the abbey. The Dissolution came in 1539, by which time the assessed income of the house had dwindled to about £118 a year. Today, the superb early 13th-century west doorway survives, and the plan of the church is clear. Notice the solid screen walls which separate the nave from its aisles. Within the transepts, the chapels retain their altar bases, and there are fine collections of floor

Medieval paving tiles at Strata Florida Abbey.

tiles. The remains of the chapter house can be seen to the south. The cloister was rebuilt at the end of the 15th century. An exhibition at the site reveals much on the history and buildings of this noble abbey.

1m ESE of Pontrhydfendigaid. C.Gb3

The 'new castle' at Swansea.

SWANSEA CASTLE, WEST GLAMORGAN

An earth-and-timber motte and bailey, the 'old castle', was raised at Swansea soon after the Norman conquest of the area by Henry de Beaumont, earl of Warwick. It became the *caput* of the lordship of Gower. This was replaced by the 'new castle', of which the ruins adjacent to Castle Gardens are the surviving remains.

A silver penny, minted at Swansea in the earlier twelfth century (By permission of the National Museum of Wales).

Talley Abbey, founded by the Lord Rhys for Premonstratensian canons in the 1180s.

The existing block lay at the southern end of a much larger stone stronghold, but appears to have developed into a self-contained castle in the late 13th or early 14th century. The remains include a hall, solar and service rooms on the first floor, with a series of vaulted basements below. The crowning glory at Swansea is the magnificent arcaded parapet around the upper walls. This was almost certainly the work of Henry de Gower, bishop of St Davids (1328-47), and recalls similar features in his palaces at Lamphey and St Davids itself. Swansea may thus have served as an episcopal palace for some time. This view has, however, recently been challenged. Some authorities now believe it is the work of the de Mowbray lord of Gower, using the bishop's masons, employed at that time elsewhere in Swansea. In the late 18th century, the northern block was re-modelled as a debtors' prison, the conditions of which became a Victorian scandal.

Near centre of city. View from surrounding areas only.   La4

TALLEY ABBEY, NEAR LLANDEILO, DYFED

Set in beautiful hills, at the head of the Talley Lakes, the abbey was founded by Rhys ap Gruffudd in the 1180s as a house of Premonstratensian (or 'white') canons. It was to remain the only monastery of this order in Wales. At its dissolution in 1536 there were some eight canons, and its income was about £136.

The remains of the central tower of the church draw the visitor from the main road. At the site, the details reveal that this church was planned on a large scale, with building progressing at the eastern end in the late 12th century. Alas, a long and costly quarrel with the neighbouring Cistercian abbey of Whitland, meant all did not go well. A much modified and reduced design in the nave tells us the ambitious scheme was never completed.

On B4302 5½m N of Llandeilo. C.   Ga6

TENBY CASTLE AND TOWN WALLS, DYFED

The castle should not be seen in isolation, for both fortress and town walls were part of an overall plan to make Tenby impregnable. Although in ruins, the castle attracts a great deal of interest because of its location on the headland overlooking the town and harbour. The castle probably dates from the mid 12th century, architectural evidence suggesting that the town walls came over a century later. The circuit of walls, remarkably well preserved in places, is the most complete in south Wales. There were four gates but of these only the West Gate, known as Five Arches, remains. The west wall is still in good condition. Nearly all of the castle walls have been removed, but enough exists to enable the area of the medieval borough to be traced without difficulty. In 1644 Tenby fell to the Parliamentarians after a fierce bombardment but later it became a Royalist stronghold.

On headland W of town centre. F. Je6

TENBY TUDOR MERCHANT'S HOUSE, DYFED

This beautifully furnished late-medieval dwelling house near the harbour of Tenby is a relic of the prosperous seafaring days of the Tudor period. Built in the late 15th century on a rectangular plan with three storeys, it has a turret projecting at the north-west corner. The original floor beams as well as many of the joists remain. During restoration, large areas of wall paintings with a design of trailing flowers similar to the Flemish weaving patterns, were discovered beneath an estimated 28 coats of

The Tudor merchant's house at Tenby.

limewash. The house is in the ownership and care of The National Trust.

On Quay Hill, opposite Bridge St. C.   *Je6*

TINKINSWOOD BURIAL CHAMBER, NEAR CARDIFF, SOUTH GLAMORGAN

Now situated in pleasant countryside a few miles west of Cardiff, a field path leads to this striking Neolithic tomb, probably built between 4,000 and 3,500 BC. It was carefully excavated in 1914 when the remains of at least 50 people of all ages were found in the rectangular chamber at the eastern end of the cairn. The massive capstone over this chamber is believed to be the largest in Britain and is estimated to weigh some 40 tons. Some of the dry-stone walling of the cairn represents modern restoration. However, its overall wedge shape, with 'horns' extending out from the entrance and forming a forecourt, is typical of the so-called 'Cotswold-Severn' group of such burial chambers.

1m S of St Nicholas, a village on A48 (T) just W of Cardiff. F.   *Ma6*

TINTERN ABBEY, GWENT

Tintern is one of the loveliest and most impressive of all the ruined British monasteries. Seen against the green wooded slopes of the Wye valley, or in the autumn against the reds and golds of the dying foliage, the abbey is justly world famous. Indeed, the valley itself, with its 'steep and lofty cliffs', has become immortalized in Wordsworth's poem 'Composed a Few Miles above Tintern Abbey'.

This was a Cistercian house, founded in 1131 by Walter fitz Richard for monks from the Norman abbey of L'Aumône. It was only the second monastery of this order in Britain, but the remote setting 'far from the habitations of men' was to become typical of the 'white monks'; a name derived from the colour of their habits. The Cistercians placed great emphasis upon manual labour, as well as the spiritual life, cultivating their own lands with the help of a special class of monks, the lay brothers. Tintern eventually built up extensive estates on both sides of the River Wye, and these were organized into compact farms, known as granges. At the Dissolution, in 1536, it was the richest abbey in Wales.

The 12th-century church and monastic buildings soon proved too small for a community growing in both status and numbers. Gradually, they were replaced after 1200 and it seems clear that few monks could have spent their entire lives free of avoiding masons' scaffolding in one or other part of the abbey. The centre of daily life at Tintern was the great abbey church, rebuilt in the late 13th century with the patronage of Roger Bigod III, and still gloriously intact. Entering at the west end, the nave was originally divided by screen walls, and it was here that the lay brothers attended services. Beyond lay the choir and presbytery, with the monks' choir stalls under the central tower and the high altar below the huge east window.

An aerial view of the Cistercian abbey at Tintern, founded in 1131.

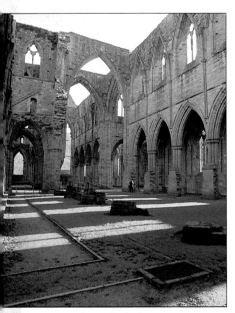

The nave in the great abbey church at Tintern.

drainage. Covered passageways ran around the four sides of this open court, and linked the domestic buildings which were arranged in a standard Cistercian pattern. The chapter house, where the monks met each day to hear a chapter of their *Rule,* lies in the east range, and there is a fine novices' lodging in this block. The choir monks' dormitory ran above these rooms. To the north, the warming house survives well, and the dining hall has evidence of a pulpit where one of the brothers read during meals. The lay brothers were accommodated in the west range. Elsewhere, to the north and west, there are the remains of the infirmary and the abbot's apartments, including a once fine 14th-century hall.

A specially designed exhibition at the site, '*Abbey in a Landscape*', tells more of the Cistercians, the monastic life at Tintern, and the

Notice the night stair down from the monks' dormitory in the north transept.

The cloister, unusually, lay to the north, perhaps for reasons of

resurrection of the site when it was first 'rediscovered' by tourists in the late 18th century. Tintern's beauty is timeless, and, standing amid the peaceful ruins, it is easy to sense the spirit which drew that very first community of monks over 850 years ago.

A selection of medieval floor tiles from Tintern Abbey (By permission of the National Museum of Wales).

Just off A466 4m N of Chepstow. C.   Me3

MONASTIC WALES

The monastic tradition in Wales went back to the earliest days of Christianity in the country, yet when the Normans arrived at the end of the 11th century they would have recognized little in the native Welsh 'monasteries'. Over the next 150 years there were to be sweeping changes, influenced not only by the new aristocracy, but also by widespread reforms in European monasticism.

To begin with, there was a strong colonist flavour in the early Norman foundations. By 1150, almost 20 Benedictine and Cluniac priories were established as dependencies of mother abbeys in England or Normandy. As at Chepstow and Pembroke, they were virtually all sited in the shadow of a castle, serving as the spiritual arm of a military conquest. By the mid 12th century, however, Wales had begun to see the effects of a proliferation of new orders intent upon introducing fresh ideals to the monastic life.

The Cistercians in particular established deep roots, with eventually 13 abbeys of the order in Wales. An important stream of foundations, springing from Whitland, flowed through the heart of native Welsh areas. Other reforming orders included the Premonstratensians, with a house founded at Talley by the Lord Rhys in the 1180s. In addition, the Augustinians made early headway in the south at Carmarthen, Haverfordwest and Llanthony, and by the early 13th century a group of important Celtic sites at Bardsey, Beddgelert and Penmon had been transformed into houses of Augustinian canons.

During the later 13th century, the monastic orders had increasingly to share their popularity with the mendicant friars. The Franciscans and the Dominicans were the most successful, with houses in a number of the larger medieval Welsh towns.

Following the Dissolution of the Monasteries under Henry VIII, some monastic churches survived to be used for parish worship. Other monastic churches and buildings were gradually plundered down to their foundations, and by the 19th century survived only as romantic ruins. Today, as outlined in this gazetteer, these ruins are precious remnants of a once unequalled architecture, and bear witness to the spiritual aspirations of the Middle Ages.

TREDEGAR HOUSE, NEWPORT, GWENT

This fine 17th-century red-bricked house, with its magnificent Restoration façade, is an example of imaginative — and timely — rescue. Renovation began in the 1970s, following a period of decline

The magnificent seventeenth-century Tredegar House.

during which Tredegar House saw use as a school. The mansion, built between 1664 and 1672, reached its *belle époque* in the mid 19th century, rising in status along with its owners, the Morgan family, who made their fortune from Newport's booming, coal-exporting docklands.

Its gilded, opulent interiors reach a high point in the State Rooms, the most stunning of which is the Gilt Room, a symphony in wood panelling bordered in gold leaf with paintings let into the upper panels. The Brown Drawing Room is no less remarkable with exquisitely carved wood panelling setting off a fine ceiling and candelabra. The house is also faithful to the memory of the servants who worked at Tredegar. The huge kitchens and rabbit warren of servants' quarters are also open to the public, in order that 'upstairs' life can be compared with that of 'downstairs'. The house stands within a 90-acre Country Park, an expansive area of beautifully tended parkland with a large lake, oak avenue, stable block, orangery and visitor centre.

1m W of Newport near M4 motorway junction 28. C. **Mc4**

Tretower Court – one of the best kept secrets in Wales.

TREFIGNATH BURIAL CHAMBER, NEAR HOLYHEAD, ISLE OF ANGLESEY, GWYNEDD

Recent archaeological excavations have revealed that this Neolithic tomb had a long and complex structural history. It began as a simple burial chamber, encased in a round cairn of boulders, at the western end of the later mound. This was then enlarged to form a wedge-shaped mound retained by drystone walls, and containing a second burial chamber. The broken capstone of this central chamber can still be seen. In the final phase, the cairn was extended further east and a third burial chamber was added. Five uprights support the great capstone of this last example. In the completed mound there was a horn-shaped recessed forecourt, which may have been the scene of elaborate rituals.

1m SE of Holyhead. F. **Aa2**

TRETOWER COURT AND CASTLE, NEAR CRICKHOWELL, POWYS

Tretower is heralded from afar by the great 13th-century round keep which rises from the valley floor. The place name is derived from this tower, but its fame lies as much in a glorious late-medieval house, as in the earlier stronghold it replaced.

An earth and timber castle was built by the Norman knight Picard, and about 1150 a stone shell keep was added to the mound. The Picard family continued to develop the site until, in the 13th century, the circular keep was added. Inside, the residential rooms have large fireplaces, but the tower and its surrounding curtain brought Tretower right up-to-date in terms of military development.

By the 14th century, peaceful times led the family to move from the cramped quarters in the round tower to the more spacious site of Tretower Court. However, it was Sir Roger Vaughan who, in the 15th

The fifteenth-century roof in Sir Roger Vaughan's north range at Tretower.

century, developed the court much as it is seen today. He rebuilt the 14th-century north range, and added the wooden gallery. Sir Roger went on to double the extent of his accommodation by building the spacious west range. The addition of the wall-walks and the gatehouse in the 1480s resulted in a plan similar to the colleges at Oxford and Cambridge. Today, the site preserves something of the flavour of gracious living in the late Middle Ages.

Generations of the Vaughans continued to live here, and the family gave literature the poet Henry Vaughan, 'the Silurist'. The last major alterations were undertaken in the 1630s when the classical-style windows were inserted around the courtyard.

3m NW of Crickhowell. C.   Mb1

Tŷ Mawr, Near Penmachno, Gwynedd

This humble cottage has great significance in the annals of traditional Welsh culture. It is the site of William Morgan's birthplace.

Bishop Morgan (*c.* 1545-1604) was the first translator of the Bible into Welsh. His translation is considered a masterpiece and is today seen as a major contribution to the survival of the Welsh language.

With its sturdy undressed stone walls and slate roof, it is a survival of a type of modest rural building in north Wales that has in most cases been altered beyond recognition. Within the cottage, there are examples of 17th- and 18th-century oak furniture.
Tŷ Mawr is in the ownership and care of The National Trust.

On minor road 2m W of Penmachno, 3½m SW of Betws-y-Coed. C.   Bb6

Tŷ Mawr the birthplace of Bishop William Morgan.

Usk Castle, Gwent

The powerful Norman lord, William Marshall (d. 1219), rebuilt this small castle, which occupies the site of an original earthwork defence. A 12th-century square stone keep survives in ruins, together with a remaining round tower (there were once three) and portions of curtain wall put up by Marshall. A gatehouse (still lived in) was added to the outer ward in the 14th century.

Reached by lane along Raglan Rd. In private ownership — admission by appointment.   Md3

The Cistercian abbey of Valle Crucis, founded in 1201.

VALLE CRUCIS ABBEY, NEAR LLANGOLLEN, CLWYD

Serene and beautiful, set in a tranquil valley beside a plentiful supply of water, Valle Crucis is a perfect Cistercian setting. The 'white monks', as they were known from their habits of undyed wool, chose to live a particularly austere form of the monastic life, and insisted upon such remote locations for their abbeys.

Valle Crucis was founded in 1201 by Madog ap Gruffudd Maelor, ruler of northern Powys, and the monks built up considerable estates in the surrounding district. By the mid 13th century they drew much of their income from wool production, and the estates themselves were worked by lay brothers. These initial ideals were severely compromised in the later Middle Ages, with the bulk of the abbey's lands and other property eventually leased to tenants. Valle Crucis suffered badly during the wars of Edward I in the later 13th century, but it continued to be a centre of Welsh culture and influence. In the 15th century, the abbey enjoyed a revival of fortunes, gaining praise from a number of poets for the quality of its buildings and the hospitality of its abbots.

The church was begun soon after the foundation, but some rebuilding and heightening took place after an apparently disastrous fire of the mid 13th century. The visitor arrives at the west front, a glorious composition, with an elaborately carved doorway added after the fire. The top section, with its rose window, is 14th century and an inscription records '*Abbot Adam carried out this work; may he rest in peace. Amen*'. Within the church, the nave was used for the lay brothers' services. Beyond the '*pulpitum*', or stone screen, the choir and presbytery to the east were reserved for the monks. Their choir stalls stood in the central crossing, with a low tower overhead. The south transept is well preserved, and its two chapels retain their altar bases. Notice the doorway high up in the south wall. From here the monks left their dormitory and descended a staircase to attend services at night. The magnificent east end of the church is best observed from outside, where there is also a surviving monastic fishpond.

The cloister lay to the south, and here the late 14th-century east range is especially well preserved. The chapter house was an important room where the monks met each day to conduct business and to listen to a chapter of their *Rule*. The upper floor was originally designed as the monks' dormitory, but in the late 15th century the northern half was converted to a fine new hall for the abbot. A chamber, with a fireplace, was built to the east and served as his private apartment. These

The rib-vaulted chapter house at Valle Crucis.

Weobley Castle, perched above the stark north Gower shoreline.

changes reflect a remarkable relaxation in the Cistercian way of life. To the south of the cloister are the remains of the monks' dining hall and kitchen. The range to the west was initially occupied by the lay brothers.

Valle Crucis was dissolved in 1537 and gradually fell into decay. In the later 16th century, however, the area formerly occupied by the abbot in the east range was converted to a private dwelling.

A very fine collection of medieval memorial sculpture is preserved in the dormitory, and there is a small exhibition revealing more of Valle Crucis and the Cistercian monastic life.

1½m N of Llangollen, close to A542 road. C.   *Ec1*

WEOBLEY CASTLE, NEAR GOWERTON, WEST GLAMORGAN

Perched above Llanrhidian marshes and the stark north Gower shoreline, Weobley has a haunting beauty which makes a visit especially memorable. The 'castle' here is best regarded as a later medieval fortified house, combining domestic comfort with a degree of much-needed security. The late 13th-century buildings were possibly begun by David de la Bere, a former steward of the de Braose lords of Gower at Swansea Castle. A John de la Bere is recorded as holding Weobley in 1432, but he seems to have been the last of that name associated with it.

The substantial remains of the buildings are grouped around a small open courtyard. On the north side is the hall, situated on the first floor, with the castle kitchens below. From the modern wooden gallery, the visitor will notice the great fireplace which warmed the hall, and the window which lit the high table where the family sat at meals. Close to this window, a door led to the solar or private rooms, set over a deep cellar. On the other side of the hall, a doorway gave access to the first-floor guest chamber. On the south of the courtyard, there is the base of a powerful square structure, which may have served as a defensible 'tower house'. Next to this, the early 14th century chapel stood on the first floor. The east range of the courtyard was never fully completed. In the late 15th century Weobley belonged to Sir Rhys ap Thomas, a courtier of Henry VII. He added the grand porch on the south side of the hall range.

The solar now houses an exhibition entitled, *Weobley: A Gower Castle and the Peninsula through the Ages*. It tells the story of Weobley, set against the colourful background of the many ancient and historic sites on the Gower Peninsula.

Off the Llanrhidian-Cheriton road, 7m W of Gowerton. C.   *Kd4*

The exhibition in the solar at Weobley Castle.

White Castle – one of the 'Three Castles' of Gwent.

WHITE CASTLE, LLANTILIO CROSSENNY, GWENT

Set deep in the Gwent countryside, White Castle takes its name from the plaster rendering that once covered the walls and towers, traces of which can still be seen. Together with Grosmont and Skenfrith, these so-called 'Three Castles' formed an important strategic triangle controlling this area of the southern March. All three were royal castles in the later 12th century, and in 1201 were granted to Hubert de Burgh by King John. Unlike the other two, however, White Castle was not rebuilt by de Burgh in the new defensive style of the early 13th century.

Today, the visitor enters the outer ward through the late 13th-century gate. Crossing the ward, a wooden bridge spans the deeply-sunk water filled moat. The twin towers of the inner gatehouse loom ahead, and from the top it is possible to enjoy a bird's-eye view of the castle and surrounding countryside. The high curtain wall can be dated to 1184–86, and the massive footings of a contemporary Norman keep can also be seen. In 1254, along with Grosmont and Skenfrith, the castle passed to the Lord Edward, the king's eldest son, and later Edward I. In 1267 it was transferred to his younger brother, Edmund, earl of Lancaster. At this time, the threatening power of Llywelyn ap Gruffudd (the Last) was at its height, and White Castle was dangerously near the frontier of his conquests. Thus, it was probably under Edward or Edmund that the gatehouse and circular towers were added as a strengthening of the defences. Indeed, overall, the castle never really functioned as a nobleman's residence, and always appears to have been more a military work. Although the internal buildings include a chapel, hall and kitchen, these seem more appropriate to a garrison commander than a great lord. Nearby is the interesting medieval moated site of Hen Gwrt.

Off B4233 at Llantilo Crossenny, 7m E of Abergavenny. C.   Md1

A thirteenth-century jug found at White Castle (By permission of the National Museum of Wales).

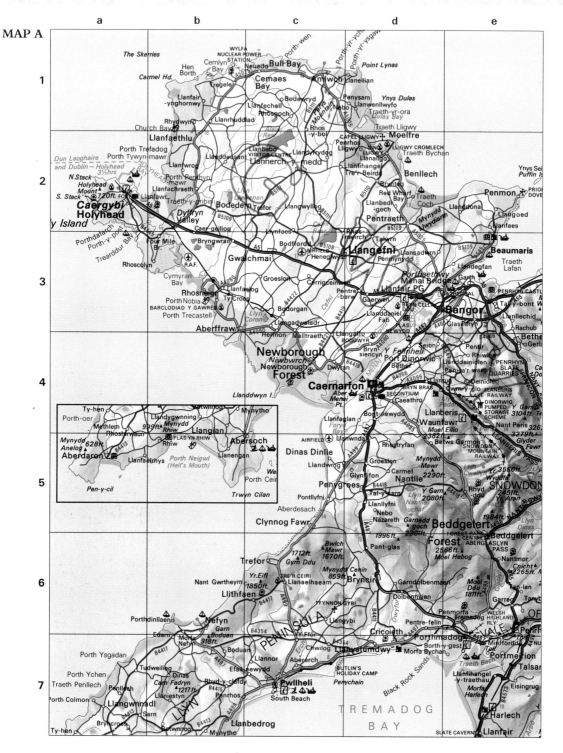

MAP A

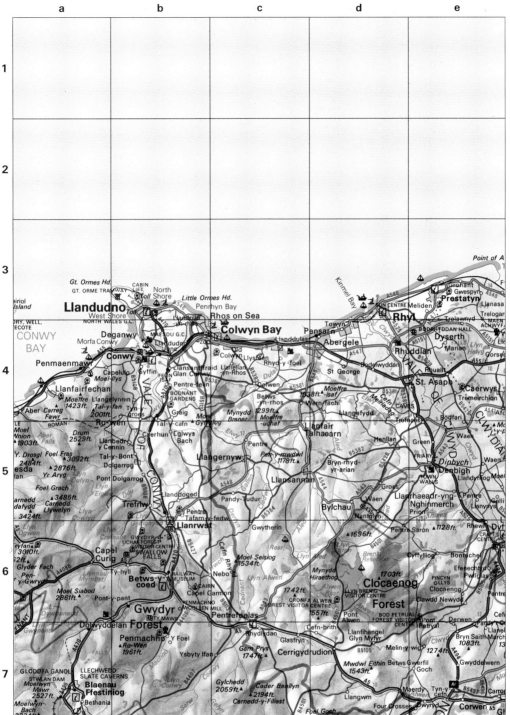

MAP C

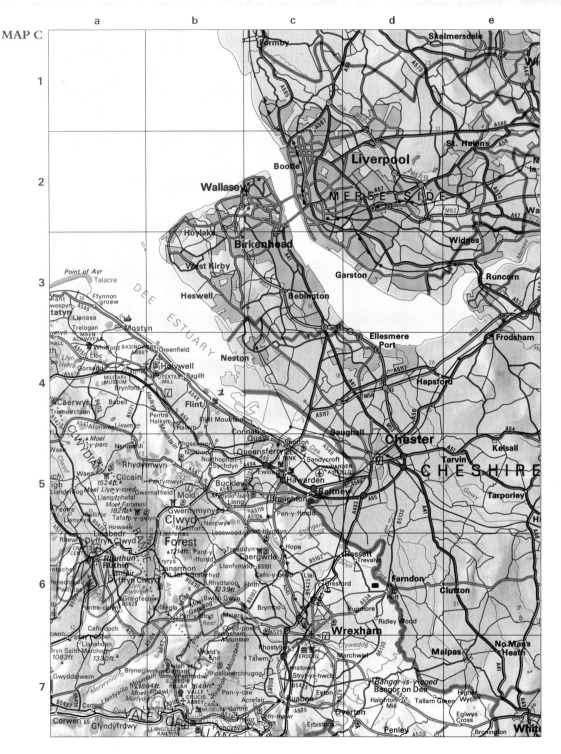

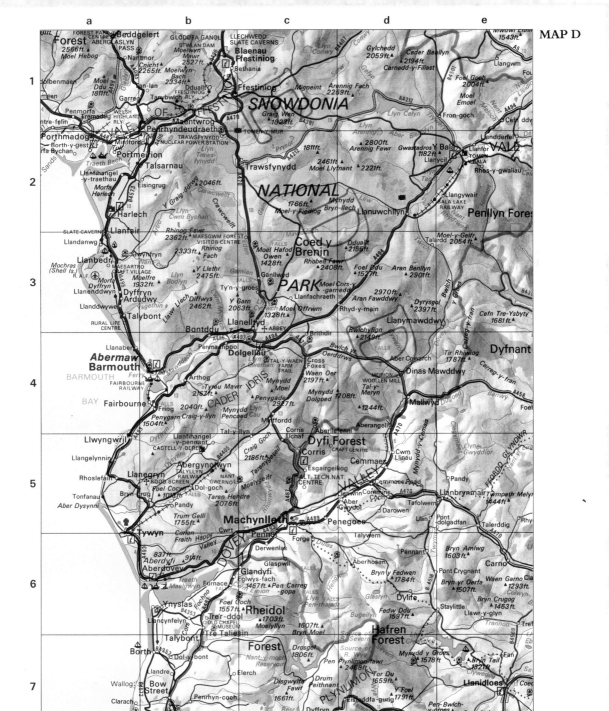

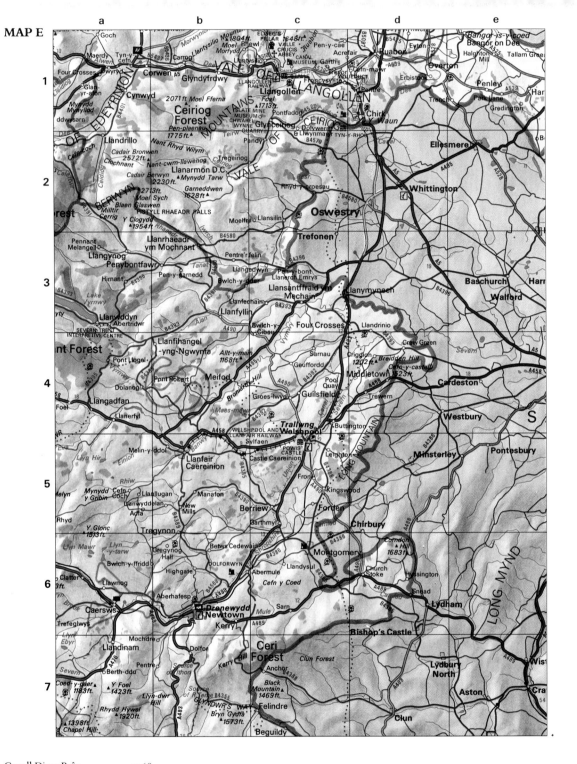

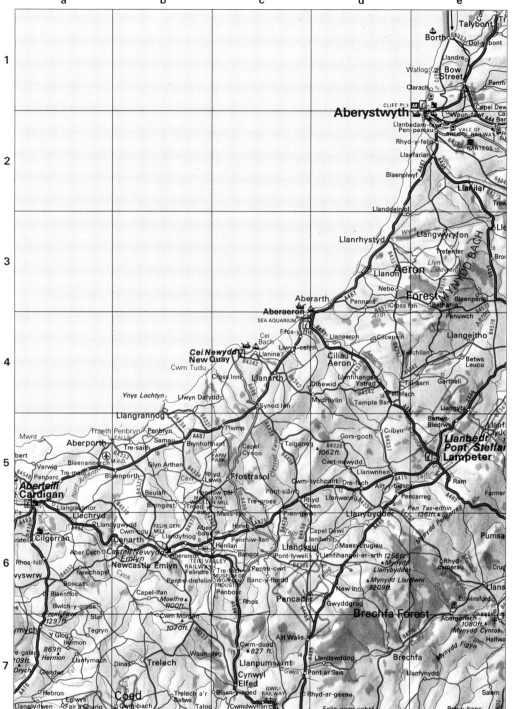

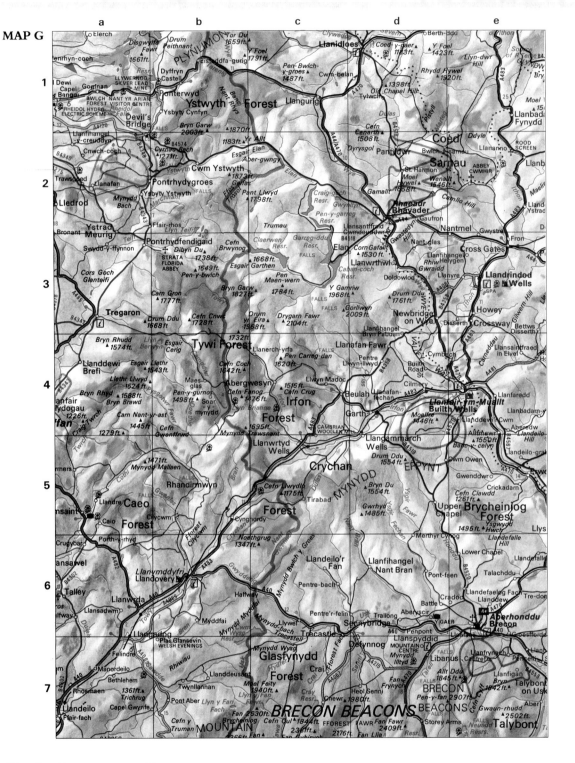

MAP G

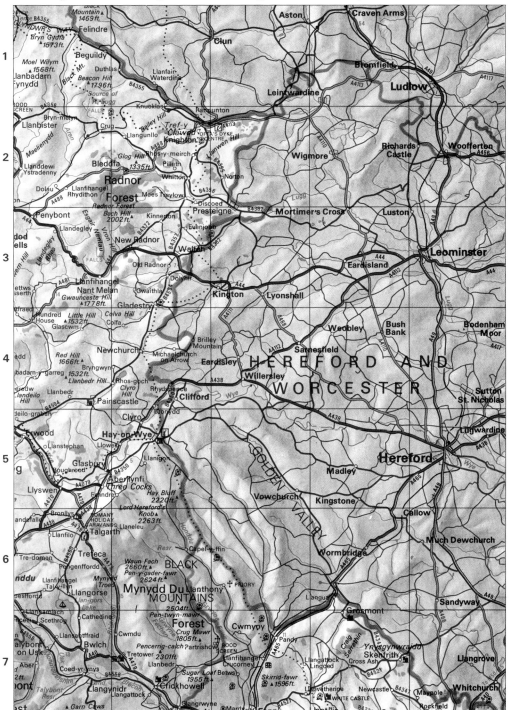

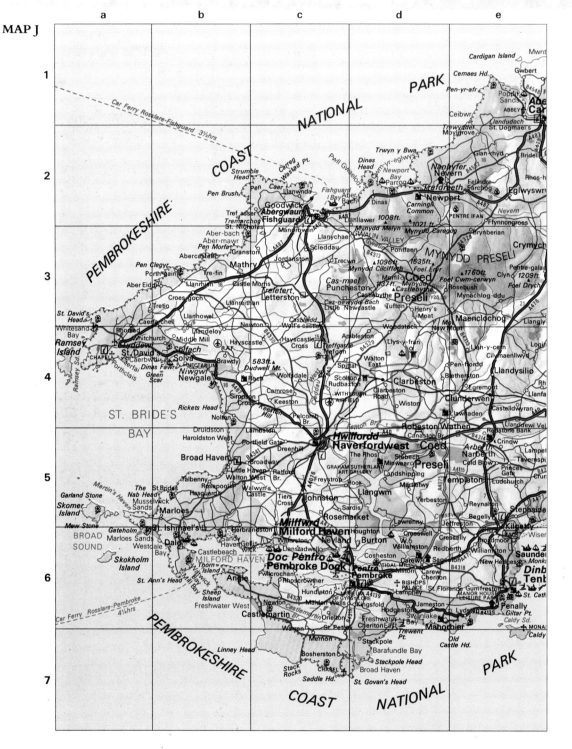

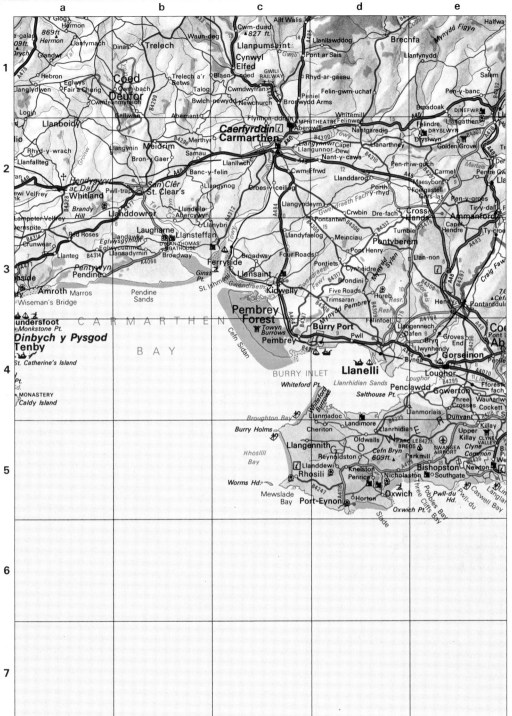

MAP L

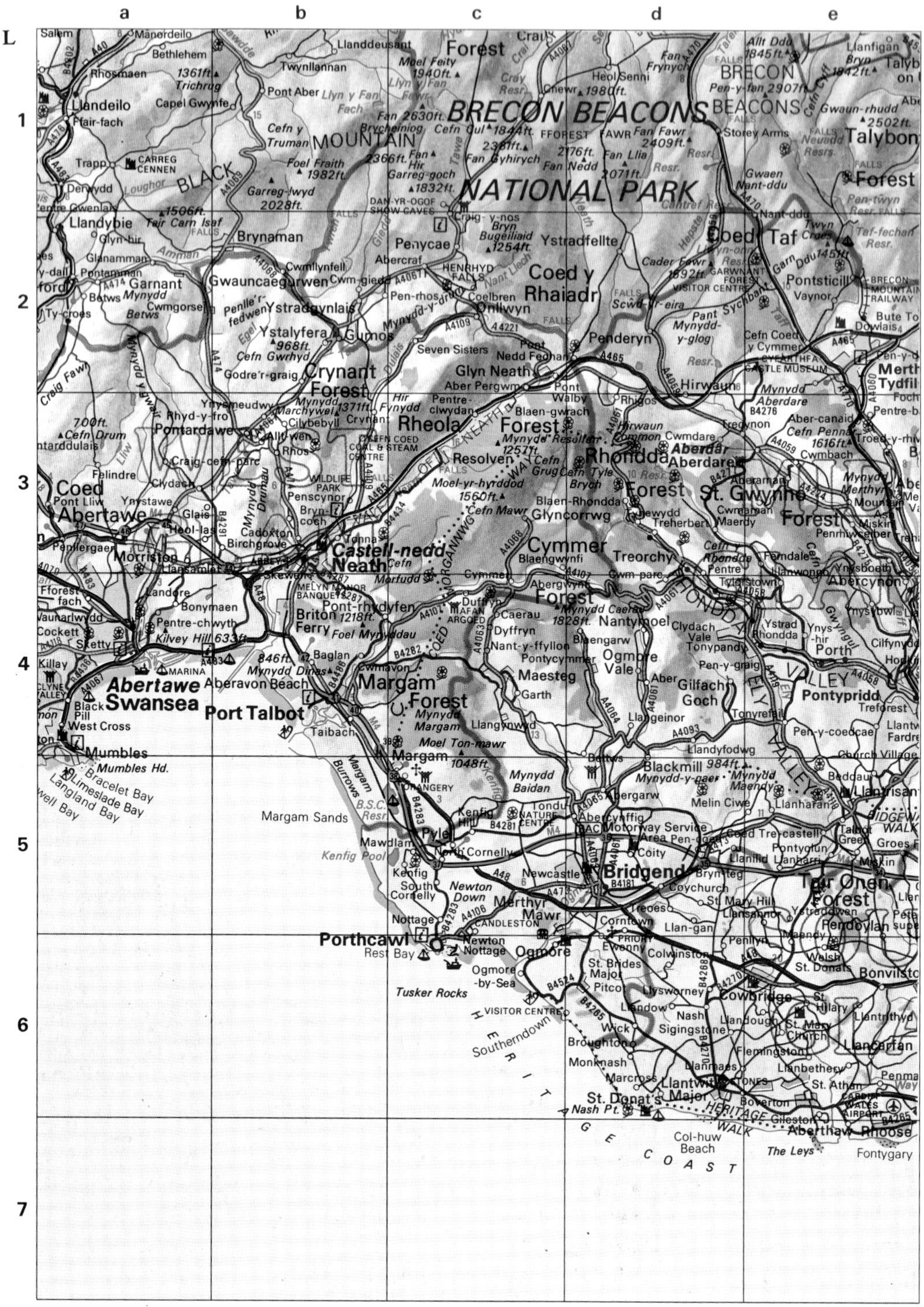